CONFIDENTIAL

MORE

FORBIDDEN KNOWLEDGE:

101 NEW THINGS NOT EVERYONE SHOULD KNOW HOW TO DO

adams
media

Published by Adams Media, an F+W Publications Company
57 Littlefield Street
Avon, MA 02322
www.adamsmedia.com

ISBN 10: 1-60550-032-1
ISBN 13: 978-1-60550-032-4

Printed in China

This publication is designed to provide accurate and authoritative information
with regard to the subject matter covered. It is sold with the understanding
that the publisher is not engaged in rendering legal, accounting, or other
professional advice. If legal advice or other expert assistance is required,
the services of a competent professional person should be sought.
—From a Declaration of Principles jointly adopted by a Committee of the
American Bar Association and a Committee of Publishers and Associations

Many of the designations used by manufacturers and sellers to distinguish
their product are claimed as trademarks. Where those designations appear in
this book and Adams Media was aware of a trademark claim, the designations
have been printed with initial capital letters.

Photographs Istockphoto.com
Illustrations by Allen Boe and Istockphoto.com
Design By Allen Boe

This book is available at quantity discounts for bulk purchases.
For information, please call 1-800-289-0963.

—————————— Dedication: ——————————

To all the people who have caught me doing horrible things.

And especially to those who didn't.

FORBIDDEN KNOWLEDGE:

101 NEW THINGS **NOT** EVERYONE SHOULD KNOW HOW TO DO

INTRODUCTION:

This really isn't a how-to book. It's a how-that's-done book. We don't expect anyone who reads this to try anything in it. In fact, we hope you don't. Much of the stuff described herein is inherently dangerous, and we'd like you to be around to purchase and read many of our other books too.

If you know how things are done, at the very least, you can guard against them being done to you. Or you can use them to make the crooks in your latest novel, comic book, or screenplay seem that much cooler and true to life.

Just please don't take any of this all that seriously. The book is meant all in fun, which you'll see as you go along. We had fun creating it. If you or anyone else got hurt because of it, that would ruin all the fun. Don't be a spoilsport. Enjoy the thrills herein vicariously. That's what books are best at.

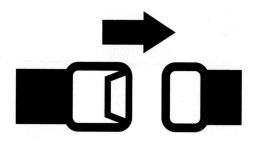

NOTICE: TO ALL CONCERNED | 00567820

CONTENTS

1. Kill a Vampire:

You've watched endless episodes of *Buffy the Vampire Slayer*, you've studied Bram Stoker's *Dracula* (including the novel, the play, the musical, the film, and even the novelization of Francis Ford Coppola's movie. You've played BloodRayne a dozen times, and the idea of a *World of Darkness* MMORPG (Massively Multiplayer Online Role-Playing Games) makes you drool. You even named the twins Jonathan and Mina.

But you don't know jack about vampires. No one does. Sure, we have dozens of legends about vampires and thousands of stories, but that's just the trouble. Not all of them can be right. And being wrong when you're facing down a thousand-year-old excuse for a human tick can be the kiss (and bite) of death.

Protective Measures

Vampires are fast, mean, and nasty, and they have the advantage of supernatural powers and potentially centuries of experience on their side. You have a handful of dusty legends (the ones you can remember) and the fact you probably won't really believe you've encountered a vampire until the moment before you're dead. (In case you're still stunned, neither of those works in your favor.)

Since you don't know for sure what you're up against, stock up on all the standards and double or triple up on them. Start with garlic, holy water, crosses, and anything else your favorite myths mention. Gather wooden stakes by the cord.

Add traditional weapons to your armory too: guns, knives, grenades, and more. Vampires are famous for making the living do their bidding, and that Super Soaker filled with holy water is only going to make such minions mad and wet.

Elimination Strategies

When you finally face down a bloodsucker, start with the simplest methods and then pile on the pain until you find something that works. Once you figure that out, hammer at it over and over until every vampire in your zip code is a pile of ash.

Most myths agree that a stake through the heart makes for a fine start for vampire extermination. In some stories, that's enough to put another notch on your cross. In *Dracula* though, a stake only pins the vampire down like a pin through a butterfly. To kill the beast, you then need to cut off its head, stuff its mouth with garlic, and cremate the remains.

If you have the time, go with the most elaborate methods. As an undead creature, the vampire has already cheated death once. You need to make sure it doesn't get that chance again. But if you're hard pressed, just stake every vampire down and then go back and finish them off properly as soon as you can.

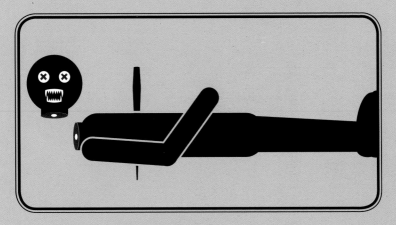

2. Beat a Breathalyzer:

You've just been pulled over on your way back home after attending Midnight Mass at St. Jude's, and you're afraid that you might have sampled a bit too much of the sacramental wine before you got behind the wheel. Father Fred might absolve your sin after a proper confession and act of contrition, but the local law isn't likely to be so forgiving.

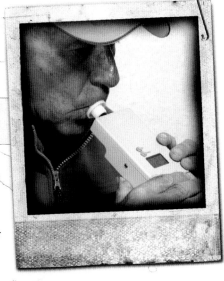

Don't Drink or Don't Drive

You don't need Oprah or MADD to tell you you're an idiot if you drink and drive, so we won't hammer that home here. Let's just say the best, most foolproof way to beat a breathalyzer is to never have to take one. If you must drive, don't drink. If you must drink, don't drive.

Can You Refuse?

Sure. The cops can't throw you to the ground and shove a breathalyzer in your mouth, then punch you in the gut until you expel your gin-soaked breath into the gadget. Well, they could, but they don't have to.

Every state has an implied consent law that says that if you have a driver's license you must consent to a breathalyzer test after being pulled over. Refusing to take one can be used against you in a court of law and often carries harsh criminal penalties of its own.

It's usually better to go along with the request and hope you're not as drunk as you fear.

What Might Work

Breathalyzers test the amount of alcohol in the air in your lungs. If you can get rid of some of that air, you might be able to reduce the amount that the breathalyzer can pick up by as much as 10%. To do this, try hyperventilating. Just don't pass out at the wheel as you do it. That won't help your case.

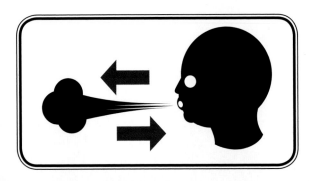

What Won't Work

Just about anything else. The most common attempts involve putting something in your mouth to try to fool the breathalyzer. People have tried pennies, mints, onions, breath spray, mouthwash, batteries, cardboard, underwear, and even their own shit.

Since the breathalyzer tests the air in your lungs instead of your mouth, none of these methods have any chance of working. In fact, some breath sprays and mouthwashes actually contain alcohol and can cause readings to look even worse.

3. Restart a Stopped Heart:

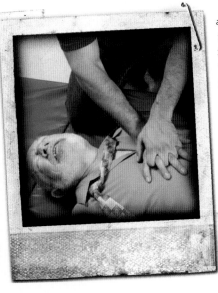

If you suddenly find yourself in a scene straight out of *Pulp Fiction* and your mob boss's girlfriend collapses to the ground with a stopped heart, what can you do? Especially if you don't happen to have a savvy drug dealer pal to hand you a needle filled with adrenaline and talk you through it?

Believe it or not, you have a number of options.

Call 9-1-1

If you don't have any clue about what to do, call 9-1-1 first. Turn on the speakerphone function on your phone, if you have one. You'll need your hands free if you want to follow the instructions of the emergency operator.

People tend to forget things in moments of stress, and this will be no exception. In a pinch, the operator might be able to help you with questions like, "How many compressions in a row in CPR?" Assuming you don't have this book with you at the time, of course.

Try CPR

The first thing most sane people would attempt in such a situation is to perform CPR. If you slept through your first-aid class (or never bothered to take one), that stands for Cardio-Pulmonary Resuscitation. "Cardio" means "heart," "Pulmonary" means "lungs," and "Resuscitation" means "getting them going again."

CPR is a series of chest compressions and breaths. Performed correctly, they can keep your friend alive until the ambulance arrives and the EMTs can take over. If you're lucky, it might even restart a stopped heart.

CPR is performed in a series of steps:

1. Tilt back the person's head and lift up the chin. This clears the airway for what happens next.

2. Blow twice into the person's mouth. This is a steady, forceful breath.

3. Put your hands in the center of the patient's chest, just above the tip of the sternum, and push down two inches. Repeat this 30 times.

4. Go back to step 2 and pray help arrives soon

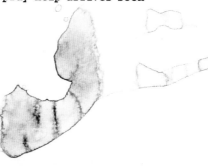

Look for a Defibrillator

Lots of public places now feature AEDs (Automated External Defibrillators). If you don't see one when you need it, ask. Stress causes people to forget they're standing next to such things.

Follow the instructions on the AED to the letter. These are designed to be easy and safe to use. Once you attach the pads to the patient, the machine analyzes the attached heartbeat and delivers a shock designed to restart it.

Don't mess around with a defibrillator just for fun. The same shock that can start a stopped heart can just as easily stop a beating heart.

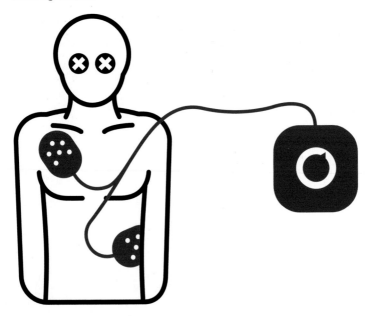

4. Walk Across a Bed of Broken Glass:

Street performers and magicians have long wowed audiences by walking or lying on all sorts of dangerous things, like hot coals or a bed of nails. Here's how to handle a bed of broken glass.

Prepare Your Own Glass

Don't just smash a bunch of beer bottles, toss off your flip-flops, and start walking around the parking lot on them. That's a recipe for disaster. Instead, wash the bottles carefully and remove the labels from them. Bottles that don't have labels—like those for Rolling Rock—make this a lot easier.

Smash the glass into tiny pieces. Remove any angled pieces or shove them to the side of the bed (the area on which you spread the glass) as you prepare for your walk. You want the edges of the glass horizontal, not vertical.

Walk Easy

Walk slowly across the glass. With each step, put your foot down flat, not heel or toe first, so that you spread your weight out over as much surface area as you can at once. Slowly rotate your foot a bit, as it lands on the glass. This helps make sure the glass beneath it is flat.

If the glass bites into you a little, do your best to ignore it. The worst thing you can do is panic and shove down harder into the glass as you try to leap away from the pain.

Concentrate and take it slow, and you should be across the glass in no time. If you have a few small cuts, be sure to show your audience the blood before you pass around the hat for their monetary applause.

Step It Up

Once you have the hang of it, you can try even dumber things. Experienced glasswalkers can carry someone on their shoulders as they go. Start with a small child and work your way up. Avoid drunks or other passengers liable to panic or be otherwise unpredictable.

You can even lie down in that same bed of glass if you like. However, doing this may not seem all that spectacular if you've just walked across the glass with a mother of five on your back. In that case, select volunteers to stand on your back as you lie face-down in the glass. Some glasswalkers have managed as many as five grown men standing on them.

Just be sure to wear a cup.

5. Defuse a Nuclear Bomb:

Usually only international super-spies have the opportunity to defuse a nuclear bomb, but if you're one such person who seems to have forgotten most of his training, then welcome back to the book, Mr. Bourne. If, on the other hand, you can't even say "nuclear," then hello, Mr. President.

Call for Help

Face it, you don't have a prayer of handling this on your own. Call 9-1-1. Ask for the bomb squad. Beg for the FBI. With luck, a squad from the Nuclear Emergency Support Team (NEST) will arrive shortly.

Remove the Detonator

If there's a timer on the bomb—you'll recognize it by the large, red numbers that count down way too fast—disconnect it. If there's any other kind of detonator, take that off instead. These are normally attached to the bomb with wires.

Unlike what you see in films, it doesn't matter which wire you cut or remove first. Cutting the power to the timer or removing any other kind of detonator should render it useless—unless it's booby-trapped. In that case, tampering with the detonator will cause the bomb to go off right away. With luck, you'll be dead before you know it.

Dismantle the Bomb

If you suspect a booby-trap, you still have options. A nuclear bomb has two major components: the radioactive material and the conventional explosives. When the bomb is activated, the explosives go off. This explosion triggers the uncontrolled nuclear reaction in the radioactive material.

So, to effectively dismantle the bomb, all you need to do is separate the explosives from the plutonium.

If you can get the explosives away from the detonator, that's the best bet. The detonator is not directly attached to the radioactive stuff. It needs the explosives for the bomb to work.

If you can't manage that, then pull the plutonium out of the bomb and hustle it away. The bomb may still go off, but then we're talking a conventional disaster, not a city-swallowing mushroom cloud.

Plutonium
Primary Device

Uranium
Secondary Device

6. Offer a Bribe:

Love might make the world go round, but money greases the gears. There are lots of reasons you might want to offer someone a bribe—an illicit offer of money, goods, or services in exchange for favorable treatment. Maybe you want to get out of a ticket. Possibly you need the health inspector to look the other way. Perhaps you need a key witness to leave town.

No matter what the reason, though, there are some guidelines you should follow when offering anyone a bribe.

Be Sly

You never know when you're dealing with someone honest, and even offering a bribe is a serious crime in most places. Unless someone flat-out demands a bribe from you, complete with an open hand, be sly about it. Come up with some thin rationale for your offer.

For instance, you might ask if you can pay a "fine" on the spot to make sure it doesn't get lost in the mail. Or you might point out that you often offer your timeshare in Florida for free to your "friends."

Not only does this give the bribee a fig leaf behind which to hide the transgression, it also gives the briber (you) some wiggle room in case you need to quickly retract the offer.

Don't Be Cheap

When you offer a bribe, you're asking someone else to put their job and perhaps even their liberty at risk for you. Unless corruption is rampant where you are—and bribes are expected, reducing the risk to near nothing—you'd better be willing to offer up something that makes taking the bribe worthwhile.

It's hard to set a price unless you're experienced with the local market for bribes. Often, you should let your new best friend do the work for you. Offer to pay a "fine" right then and there, or offer to share something you have with the friend and let him figure out how much he can take before you protest.

7. Pull Off a Short-Change Scam:

Imagine you're working the register at the local Kwik-E-Mart, and a woman walks in and buys a cheap pack of gum that costs 79 cents. You ring it up, and she hands you a ten-dollar bill. You hand her back nine dollar bills, two dimes, and a penny.

The woman pockets the coins, then says, "Wow, I don't want to carry all that change. Can I give you ten ones back for my ten-dollar bill?"

Being a bastion of good customer service, you agree. She hands you the money, and you hand her a ten-dollar bill.

Counting the money before you put it back in the register, you see that she's given you nine ones and a ten, $19 instead of the $10 you had coming. You point this out, and she blushes at the mistake. "I'll just add another dollar to that, and you can give me a twenty, all right?"

Kind and gentle soul that you are, you agree again. She smiles as she walks out the door.

Later, as you close out your register, you discover that
you're $10 short.

How Did That Happen?

It's simple. When the woman handed you $19, $10 of that
should have gone straight into your register. That's what you
just gave her the ten-dollar bill for, right?

If you had given her back the extra $9, you would have been
set. Instead, you let her confuse you into forgetting you'd
already given her $10 for that $19. When she chips in another
dollar and you hand her a twenty, she's now given you $20 in
exchange for $30. (That's the first $10 you gave her, plus the
final $20.)

When you try to pull of the scam, always finish one transaction before you start another. It's the melding of what should
be two separate deals into one that messes many people up.

8. Get Away with Speeding:

This one's easy: Don't drive any faster than the speed limit.

If you're a modern-day Sammy Hagar (although perhaps one who's updated "I Can't Drive 55" to reflect today's speed limits), the idea of restraining yourself for the safety and convenience of others may pale against the thrill of recreating the finest scenes of *The Fast and the Furious*. If so, there are some ways to have your thrills and avoid complications with the law.

1. Get a Radar/Laser Detector. Attach one of these handy, little devices to your windshield or dashboard (unless you're in someplace they're illegal, like Virginia or D.C.), plug it into your car's cigarette lighter socket, and you're ready to go. They detect the output from the radar and laser guns police officers use to clock speeders. If you're lucky, you'll catch a bounce off a car in front of you before the trooper targets you. This only gives you an instant's warning to hit your brakes, though, so if you're driving too fast they won't keep you from getting a ticket, just reduce the amount of your fine.

2. Drive slower. Most cops want to nail big offenders, those going 20 or more miles per hour over the limit. That's when "reckless driving" laws kick in automatically too, compounding the fines. If you stick to driving only 10 or 15 miles per hour over the limit, you lower your profile—and your fine if a bored trooper decides you're worth his while after all.

3. Get a Radar Jammer. These transmit on a frequency designed to foil a radar detector. They are illegal in most areas, though, and they don't prevent a cop from spotting how fast you're moving by eye. Then he can just pick you up via NASCAR. (That's cop slang for following a speeder and gauging his speed by checking your own speedometer.)

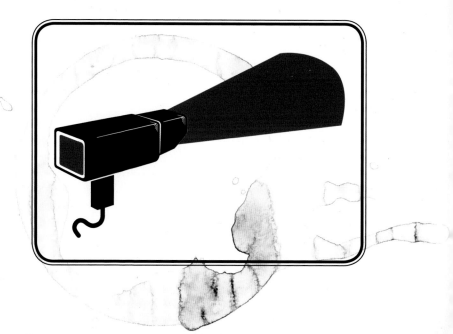

9. Beat a Traffic Ticket:

Just because a cop caught you speeding doesn't mean you'll get a ticket.

Talk Your Way Out of It

When you're pulled over, take out your license and your registration and have them ready. Speak politely and apologetically to the nice officer and offer up any extenuating circumstances you may have. Be careful though. If you say you're heading for the hospital because your wife is in labor, you may receive a police escort that takes you far out of your way.

If you're an attorney, judge, politician, or otherwise connected, hand the cop your business card along with your license. Cops like to give tickets to people who aren't inclined to fight them or get them fixed. It saves them the hassle of appearing in court or getting a phone call from their boss.

Go to Court

Even if you're guilty, find an attorney who specializes in traffic law to help you out. The attorney knows the law and—just as importantly—the local district attorney and judges. With luck, she'll be able to save you the hassle of appearing in court at all.

If you can't afford a lawyer, go to court yourself. If you have a relatively clean record, you can explain yourself to the judge and ask for mercy.

If you or your attorney makes a good impression, the charges against you may be reduced or even eliminated. A speeding ticket can be changed to obstructing traffic, for instance. Or the judge or DA may ask you to make a donation in a certain amount to an established charity of your choice.

(Donating to a charity of someone else's choice—like that of the judge or DA granting you clemency—could be considered a bribe. That's why you get to make the choice. If you'd like to be able to use this option again in the future, don't donate to the campaign fund of the DA's opponent—unless you're sure you're backing a winner.)

10. Lie Effectively:

There are lots of ways to spin untruths, but many people get caught lying all the time. Here are ten tips to make you a better liar.

1. Relax. Nervous people seem like they're lying even when they're not. If you want someone to believe your lie, it's more about how you say it than what you say.

2. Tell people what they want to hear. People are more likely to believe a lie if you tell them what they would rather hear from you. It's even better if it's what they expect to hear.

3. Keep close to the facts. The fewer points at which you deviate from the truth, the easier it is to keep your story straight.

4. If you can't go small, go big. If there are any outrageous truths you can toss into your lie, use them. Give your audience something they can't believe to be true and then prove it's so. This makes it easier for a listener to swallow the rest of the story.

5. Look people in the eye. Liars tend to evade direct eye contact.

6. Deny, deny, deny. Put the burden of proof on those who call you a liar. Make them prove their accusations. It's a lot harder to do than most people think.

7. Switch the subject. If someone manages to prove you lied about something, change the course of the conversation to something else. State that the lie is trivial, the product of a mistake rather than malice, and that it's beside the (new) point anyhow.

8. Suffer from memory loss. If the event you need to lie about is further in the past than a few hours back, repeat this phrase: "I can't recall." It worked for the Gipper and a good chunk of the Bush administration. It can work for you.

9. Split hairs. Play with the definitions of words. Bill Clinton raised such prevarication to an art form when arguing about "what the meaning of the word 'is' is."

10. Establish an alibi. Get your friends to lie for you. This is especially effective if you're all involved in the same lie and are lying for each other. Chances that any of you will crack drop dramatically.

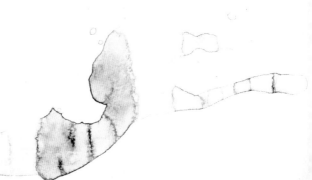

11. Get Elected Effortlessly :

Maybe you want to do some good for your community. Or possibly you'd rather accept bribes than be giving them. Or it could be you have plans to launch a preemptive war at the first excuse. No matter what your reason, here are a few tips for how to get yourself elected.

1. Have a lot of friends, preferably of legal voting age. These are the people who can legitimately stuff the ballot box with votes for you. Court them well.

2. Have wealthy friends. Modern campaigns cost a lot of money. The total cost of this year's Presidential campaign should top a billion dollars. Somebody has to pay for all that.

3. Be rich. If you can't get enough people to donate to your campaign quickly enough, you can always spend your own money to get elected instead. You can just call it a "loan" so you can pay yourself back if you do eventually line up enough donors.

4. Hack the electronic voting machines. Machines that leave no paper trail to prove their tallies are ripe for the plunder.

5. Bring out the dead. Just because some of your staunchest supporters have passed on doesn't mean you can't rely on their votes.

6. Intimidate voters. Send lawyers down to local polling places to challenge the credentials of every voter—that isn't voting for you.

7. Have friends in high places. In case of a close count, the ballot may be decided in the court. Having friends on the court can come in handy—especially if your father appointed enough of them in the first place.

8. Go negative. Who cares if you're the best person for the job? Just make sure everyone thinks your opponent is the worst.

9. Fight for it. Win a war. Everyone loves a winner—or at least someone who hasn't lost yet.

10. Get the most votes. If you amass enough of a margin of victory, this should foil all of your opponent's dirty tricks—in theory.

12. Become a Brewmaster :

As Ben Franklin said, "Beer is proof that God loves us and wants us to be happy." People have been making and brewing beer for thousands of years, since the dawn of civilization. Coincidence? Of course not!

Home Brewing

The easiest way to brew your own beer is to pick up a kit. This is much like a cake mix except you can get drunk on the results. Most homebrew kits come with a set of starter ingredients, some kind of container in which you can let the beer brew or ferment, and a set of bottles into which you can pour the beer when it's ready.

If you know what you're doing, you can manage without all of these things, but that's sort of like making a frozen margarita without a blender. It's possible, but the extra effort takes the fun out of it.

The Ingredients

To make beer, you only need four things: water, some kind of starch to ferment (usually malted barley), hops, and yeast. For flavor, most brewers add various flavors. Try mixing in things you like.

Find the best ingredients you can. You'll blow your first batch or two badly, but there's no reason to blame it on bad hops.

Making Beer

This is a simple, five-step process:

1. Steep the malted barley in hot water. This gets the sugars moving and produces a mash.

2. Remove the solid bits from the mash, and you're left with a wort (sugary water).

3. Add the hops in and boil the wort, reducing the water in it.

4. Add yeast to the wort and leave it for a few weeks. The yeast turns the sugars in the wort into alcohol.

5. Bottle it up. Some people add a bit more wort or sugar here so that the yeast can carbonate the beer a bit more too. Don't let it sit for too long after this, or the pressure in the bottles can build to the point at which they can burst.

5. Drink up.

13. Waterboard a Terrorist:

There's been a lot of debate about whether or not certain practices the US Government has approved for use in the War on Terror constitute torture. The most contentious of these is waterboarding, originally known as the Chinese water torture. This causes a victim to feel like he's drowning but in theory does no direct physical harm—other than potentially causing a stroke, heart attack, or other catastrophe from the stress.

The Catholic Church apparently used waterboarding in the Spanish Inquisition, and it's been a favorite interrogation tool ever since, used by groups ranging from the Gestapo to the Khmer Rouge. Today, members of the US special forces undergo waterboarding as part of their survival school training.

Here's how it's done.

1. Strap the victim down on his back. Traditionally, this involves immobilizing him on a board (thus the name of the technique), but anything that holds him down should do.

2. Raise the victim's feet so they are higher than the head.

3. Cover the victim's face or stuff a rag into his mouth. You can use a cloth for this, although some have used cling wrap with a hole pierced for the mouth.

4. Pour water over the victim's face.

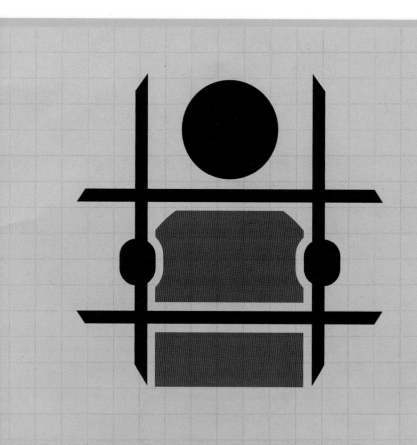

How It Works

The water induces the gag reflex and causes the victim to feel like he is drowning. Reportedly even CIA agents cannot endure this for longer than 15 seconds.

How to Get Away with It

If you're a private citizen and get caught doing this, the police will want to have a long chat with you, followed by a long visit in the appropriate lock-up. If you're part of the CIA or the US military, you may find that your superiors have granted you limited permission to use this technique, despite the fact that US soldiers and officers faced court-martial charges for doing so in both the Vietnam and Spanish-American Wars.

14. Cheat at Gambling:

There are many different ways to cheat at gambling, but the idea behind them all is the same: to take the money of the other players without letting them know you're cheating. If you want to rob someone, it's simpler to just mug him—and possibly more honest.

There are three main ways to cheat at gambling.

1. Skilled cheats. This is the classic kind of cheating you see in all sorts of films and shows. It involves things like palming cards, controlled rolling, dealing from the bottom of the deck, or having the infamous ace up your sleeve. This is a difficult way to cheat, as it requires a lot of practice. Also those who perform such tricks usually know how to spot them.

2. Mechanical cheats. If you can't rely on skill, then go for ingenuity instead. Some cheats mark decks by edging cards with a fingernail or bending a corner of a card, while others swap out the regular dice for loaded ones.

You can even find decks with coded patterns buried in the designs on their backs, designed so that only those who know the patterns are likely to even see them.

3. Teamwork. Most card games are built on the premise that each player only knows the content of his own hand. Players who somehow share information can turn the odds in their favor. This is why table talk is usually discouraged.

Casinos Can Cheat Too

If any player can cheat, there's little (outside of gambling regulators and savvy players) to keep casinos from doing so too. In the case of large casinos in big cities like Las Vegas, there's the threat of losing a reputation as an honest house too, but for smaller operations that's less of a disincentive.

Some such places can use a shoe (a device used in a casino to hold several decks of cards shuffled together) rigged to keep the top card (usually a face card) in place until the dealer wants it. Others might have a craps table with a foot-activated electromagnet built into the base. Couple this with a set of dice with iron filings mixed into the paint on one face of each die, and you have a system that's hard to spot and impossible to beat.

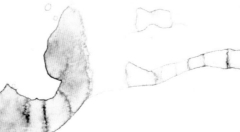

15. Get Out of Handcuffs:

If you happen to find yourself bound with your hands behind your back, you're likely in a heap of trouble. If you've been arrested by the police, your best bet is to leave the handcuffs on. Removing them could be construed as resisting arrest or an attempt to escape, both of which are serious charges to add on to whatever you were arrested for in the first place.

If you have some other good reason to remove handcuffs, though, here's how.

Pick It

The locks on most handcuffs are fairly simple. This is one reason your hands are usually placed behind your back when you're cuffed. It's hard to undo a lock you can't see, even if you happen to somehow have a key.

Assuming you don't have a key, look for a piece of wire with which you can fashion a crude lockpick. A bobby pin works well for this, once you strip off the plastic bits on the end. In a pinch (like what you're probably in), you can use a paperclip.

Bend the end of the wire at a right angle about a quarter inch from its end. Then, about halfway back to the top, bend it back in the original direction. Push this into the lock. Use the bend to shove down the little post in the center of the lock, then twist your pick around until the lock opens.

Shim It

Handcuffs resize automatically to fit their captives by means of serrated teeth that go through a one-way ratchet. If you have a thin, stiff piece of wire—say the tip of a safety pin—you may be able to shim the ratchet open. To do this, slip this between the teeth and the ratchet. If done correctly, the cuffs should easily pull off your wrists.

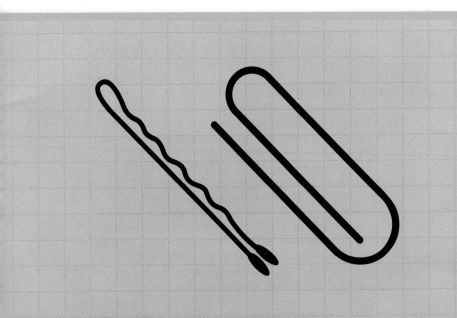

Slip Free

If you have nothing from which you can fashion a pick or a shim, you can try to get free the old-fashioned way and just slip your wrists out of the cuffs. If they've been put on properly, this can be a difficult trick, and even trying it can cost you some skin around your wrists.

If possible, rub lubricant of some kind on your skin and the cuffs to help you slip free. Petroleum jelly is brilliant for this, but any kind of liquid—from spit to plain water—can help.

16. Take a Tasing:

If you've decided to take up asking impertinent questions of former Presidential candidates, you might find yourself facing a top of the line stun gun known as a Taser. While cops usually hesitate to pull out a pistol and shoot someone who's resisting being duck-walked out of a place, they may be happy to stun them long enough to get the troublemaker out of the room.

Stay Away

A Taser uses compressed gas to fire a pair of barbed metal probes at a target. These are attached to the weapon by a pair of wires. The wires only have a short range—usually about twenty feet. If someone threatens you with a Taser, back up. If you can't manage that, hide behind something solid, like a table or a door.

The first Taser models struggled to penetrate thick clothes, but that's not true of the newer versions. The probes don't even have to touch your skin. If they get close enough, they can zap you right through your clothes.

Just One Shot

The real weakness of a Taser is that it's only good for a single shot at a time. If the shot missed, the user has to rewind and repack the wires, plus load in a new compressed gas cartridge.

Ka-Zap!

If you happen to find yourself hit by a Taser, good luck. It doesn't much matter how tough you are or how much pain you can tolerate. On a successful hit, a Taser shoots 50,000 volts through your body for five seconds.

The electric pulse causes all of the muscles in your body to contract at once. This is both painful and paralyzing. Once it's over, you may recover right away, but this often depends if you fell over while paralyzed—and how you landed.

Stay Still

If you've been tased once, lie down and stay still. As long as the barbed darts are still in you, all the guy with the Taser has to do is squeeze the trigger once more to zap you again. Struggling or even moving only invites such action.

Even if you somehow manage to tear out the probes before the attacker can zap you again, most Tasers have built-in electrodes in addition to the probes. These can be used by just touching you, and if you've been hit once the attacker can easily get close enough to zap you again by hand.

Since the turn of the century, nearly 200 people have died after being tased. While Tasers are far safer for targets than guns, they are serious weapons and should be treated with respect.

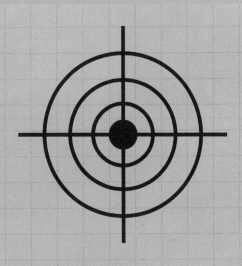

17. Survive Getting Shot At:

It's a hard world out there, and it's getting harder every day. With the rise of incidence of school and workplace shootings, it pays to know what to do if someone goes postal near you.

1. Hide. The best defense against a shooter is to make sure he never finds you. Look for a good spot he wouldn't suspect: under a desk, in a supply closet, in the trunk of a car, inside a cabinet, and so on.

2. Duck. If you hear gunshots or see a shooter, duck behind something opaque and preferably solid. The more solid it is, the better. High-caliber bullets go right through a hollow-core, wooden door, but they bounce off thick steel.

3. Cover. If you can do nothing else, try to cover your head and chest. You can survive a shot to the arm, but one that goes through your head is far more likely to be fatal.

4. Hit the Dirt. Standing targets have a better chance of being seen and shot at. Also, if you're trying to avoid a sniper, lying prone usually makes you a smaller target.

5. Run. If you think you can escape, high-tail it out of there. If you're in a building, find the nearest exit (either a door or window) and use it. Running away from a shooter across an open field is a loser's game—unless you have no other choice. If you must do so, juke back and forth as you go to make it harder to be hit.

6. Phone for Help. First chance you get, call 9-1-1. Even if you cannot speak, leave the connection open. If you're on a landline, the 9-1-1 dispatcher should be able to find your location and send help. The same goes for most cell phones—unless you've disabled the GPS signal yours gives out.

7. Lock the Door. If you're fortunate enough to have a door between you and the shooter when the bullets start flying, lock it. Then step away from it in case he tries to blast through it. If the door doesn't have a lock, barricade it with heavy furniture or jam a chair up under the doorknob.

8. Keep Quiet. You don't want to attract the shooter's attention. Hollering for help or crying out loud may only show him where you're hiding. Don't scream for help.

9. Talk Him Down. If you know the shooter well and think you might be able to talk him into stopping with the bullets, you can give it a try. Keep in mind, though, that's he's already started shooting and may be far beyond reason of any kind. You may only be inviting him to shoot at you.

10. Attack. This should be your last resort. Only attack the shooter if you must or if a golden opportunity presents itself. Rushing a man with a gun is rarely a good idea, especially if he's already shown he's ready to shoot. If possible, ambush the shooter instead, striking from behind. Grab the barrel of the gun and push it away from yourself. Then fight as dirty as you can. There are no rules to stop you.

18. Survive Getting Shot:

If you somehow manage to find yourself on the wrong end of an active firearm, you're likely in for a world of pain. Just because you've been shot, though, doesn't mean you're dead. Here are some tips for how to survive.

Don't Get Shot Again

If you're lucky, this was an accidental shooting, and you're surrounded by many scared and apologetic people who want to help you. If that's not the case, do whatever you can to avoid being shot again. If you're too injured to escape or hide, try playing dead. Unless the shooter really wants you dead, he might not waste any more bullets on you.

Call for Help

If the shot didn't instantly kill you, the biggest danger is that shock or blood loss will do you in before anyone else can get to you. Rather than risk that happening while you make your way to the nearest doctor, call 9-1-1 and have them come to you. They should also call the police, which may help you with the problem of the shooter.

Find the Wound

You're probably in shock or pumped full of adrenaline. You may not even realize just where the wound is, only that you've been hit. If you can, take off any clothing covering the wounded area and check all around. (That shirt's been ruined anyway, and you can use it in the next step.)

Once you find the wound, look for others. You may have been shot more than once. Also, look on the other side of your body from the wound. You may discover that you have an exit wound: another hole in you from where the bullet left screaming through your body.

Stop the Bleeding

You need to keep as much of your blood inside of you as you can. Apply direct pressure to the wound to stop the flow of blood. Use a cloth for this if you can, but even your bare hand is better than nothing.

If direct pressure doesn't work, try pressing on the artery supplying blood to the area. If that doesn't help either, try a tourniquet. Using a tourniquet might mean sacrificing a limb, but it beats dying.

Leave the Bullet

Unless you're an ER doctor, taking out the bullet will likely do more harm than good. The bullet acts as a partial plug atop the damage it's done to you. If you pull it out, you remove the plug, and the blood might flow even faster.

Get to a Hospital

If you haven't been able to call for help, go find it instead. If possible, have someone else drive. Passing out at the wheel from blood loss can be as fatal as any gunshot.

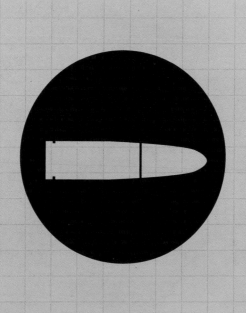

19. Navigate a Minefield:

Let's say you're a journalist who's wandering around the mountains of Afghanistan hunting for Taliban to interview. You're hiking up to a remote village and are about to ask your guide how much farther it could possibly be when an explosion sprouts from under his feet and he disappears in a cloud of gunpowder and blood.

You realize that you should have paid for the more experienced guide rather than trying to save your boss a few bucks. Now you're in the middle of a minefield. How do you get out?

Stop Moving

Freeze. Don't make another move until you can assess the situation. A hasty move in any direction could kill you.

Look for a Safe Path Out

The only path you know is safe for sure is where you've already walked. If possible, walk backward into your own footsteps until you are positive you're safe.

If that's not possible, look for another path. You might see where people or animals have successfully negotiated a way through the mines. Stick to these if you can.

Keep Sharp

Peel your eyes for freshly turned dirt, trip wires, spikes, lumps, different soil colors, or other irregularities in the ground around you. Avoid these areas.

Use an Animal

If you have an animal around you, send it the way you figure is the shortest way out of the minefield. Then follow it from a safe distance, stepping exactly in its tracks—or as close as you can manage. This sort of trick only works once per animal though, so take as much care as you can.

Fall Back

Some mines detonate not when you step on the mine but when you step off it. If you step on something and feel it click, you may have found such a mine. In any case, you may have up to a second before the mine goes off. Throw yourself to the ground behind you, your feet toward the expected detonation. You won't be able to outrun the explosion, but you can cover up and protect as much of yourself as possible.

Five Things to Not Do

1. Don't use a probe to find a mine. If you're close enough to set it off, it's close enough to hurt you—or detonate a mine that's closer to you.

2. Don't use a two-way radio to call for help. Their frequencies can detonate some mines. A cell phone might too, although this is less common.

3. Don't voluntarily detonate a mine if you're anywhere near the minefield. You might cause a chain reaction that could kill you.

4. Don't depend on a metal detector. Mines can be made of non-metallic material.

5. Don't try to defuse or disarm a mine—unless you really know what you're doing.

20. Pirate Copyrighted Files:

Information wants to be free, right? In one sense, that's true. People who use information want to be able to do so when and where they like, without the troubles that digital rights management (DRM) causes.

For instance, have you every tried to play a song with DRM from iTunes on an MP3 player other than an iPod? It can't be done.

Well, of course it can be done. Just not legally.

Burn and Rip

The easy way around this is to burn a CD of your DRM'd songs. Then you can reinsert the disc and rip the songs off it to your music library just as if they were on a store-bought CD.

This, however, is a pain in the ass.

P2P Networks

Once you're ready to ignore copyright laws entirely and stick it to the RIAA (Recording Industry Association of America), you need to tap into one of the more popular peer-to-peer networks out there, like Gnutella or BitTorrent. For this, you just need to grab a program like Acquisition on the Mac, or BitTorrent, or LimeWire on Windows.

Once you get on the P2P Network, just search for whatever you like, from the latest Britney Spears album to your favorite porn films. Then set your program to download the goodies and wait for the files to appear on your computer.

With BitTorrent, you need to find a Torrent file first. Fortunately, there are search engines on the web that make this easy, like ThePirateBay.com. Once you have this file, you simply open it with your BitTorrent client and use it.

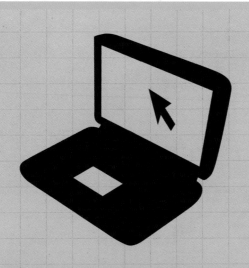

Legal Concerns

While pirates (those who download files illegally) may want
information to be free, the same isn't true of those who
create that information or publish it. These folks want to
be paid for their efforts, and many of them view pirates as
direct threats to their livelihoods.

There's an ongoing debate about whether or not freely available files help or hinder actual sales numbers. Despite that,
the RIAA and MPAA (the equivalent organization for producers
of movies) have taken strong legal action against pirates of
all stripes. (Whether or not this is always legitimate or wise
is the subject of another set of debates.) Fines can be up to
$150,000 for each song traded illegally. Keep that in mind when
deciding just how free "free" music might be.

— 21. Enjoy Bondage:

Bondage is technically the use of restraints for pleasure—generally sexual pleasure. It does not have to, but can, include spanking, ball gags, light torture, controlled pain, chocolate syrup, or the all-too-appropriately named whipped cream.

Bondage is not for everyone, but a good and growing number of people seem to enjoy it. If you're thinking of tossing a few ropes or a set of handcuffs into your bed to see what might happen, here are a few tips to get you started.

Start Slow

Don't jump straight into full-leather bodysuits covered with zippers over every orifice and D-rings for restraint clips. Go easy and see how you like it. Start tying each other up with bandanas and work your way up to ropes and handcuffs later on. (See the entry on how to "Get Out of Handcuffs" if you're not too sure about all this.)

Build Trust

Find a partner you think you can trust and then build that trust over time. It's hard to enjoy bondage if you're really scared that something horrible might happen to you. It's supposed to be for fun, so pick someone who you think you can have that kind of fun with and then take your time to find out if you're right.

Safety First

Bondage, like a lot of sexual play, often features a healthy bit of roleplaying. The one being held might be expected to beg for release and might be pretty convincing about it. To help both people (or everyone!) involved to feel good about this, establish a safe word before you start.

This word should be something that wouldn't normally come up during conversation—especially as part of the kind of talking that goes on during bondage. When anyone says it, the bondage has to end immediately, and those who are bound must be released. Ignoring a safety word is a terrible taboo in bondage. If you violate that trust, you may find it harder to find some play in the future.

22. Read the Necronomicon:

The *Necronomicon* is the Book of the Dead, a tome that contains all sorts of forbidden knowledge about the afterlife and the creatures who call that place home. It has its roots in the Egyptian burial tomes found either inscribed on scrolls or engraved on the walls of tombs, but it's been popularized in more modern entertainment as something far, far worse.

In his short story "The Hound," H.P. Lovecraft came up with the modern version of the book, a fictional tome written by the "Mad Arab" Abdul Alhazred. Other authors of the time, friends of Lovecraft, cited the book in their own stories, and over time many readers came to think the book was real. Since then, many books have been published under the title *Necronomicon*, most claiming to be the book Lovecraft "referenced."

Finding the Necronomicon

If you happen to wind up like Bruce Campbell's character Ash in the classic horror flick *Evil Dead* and stumble across an ancient book bound in real human-skin, put it down and walk away. Seriously. No good can come of this.

If you're smart, you'll call the feds and hope they have something like the BPRD (The Bureau for Paranormal Research and Defense) from *Hellboy* ready to roll. You'll get swept away, decontaminated, debriefed, and perhaps exorcized. Then you'll get to go on with your life as if nothing had ever happened.

If you're the curious type, though—or just figure you've found a particularly gruesome fake—then, well, you're wise but doomed.

Reading the Necronomicon

Don't do it.

All right, you opened the (literally) damned book up, and it's too late. You've already got ideas shambling around in your head that "man was not meant to know." You have two options.

1. Walk away and endure years of therapy and perhaps institutionalization while you try to forget the horrible things you've learned.

2. Keep reading and hope that you can learn something useful in the book that could help you with your brand-new problem of creeping insanity brought on by knowledge of (again, literally) mind-blowing subjects.

Either way, you'll end up either dead or stark, raving mad. Or both.

In either order.

23. Learn about the Old Ones:

Now that you've gotten a taste for the particular flavor of madness inspired by the *Necronomicon*, you might want to do some further research. Just because you've started down the long, slippery slope toward insanity doesn't mean you shouldn't find yourself a toboggan and enjoy the ride.

The Old Who?

H.P. Lovecraft created a pantheon of ancient, uncaring gods often referred to in general as the Mythos. Other authors have contributed to this group over the years, and it continues to grow in this apocryphal way. The most notorious of these creatures is the great Cthulhu, a gigantic creature with bat wings and an octopus for a head. Think Davy Jones from the *Pirates of the Caribbean* films, only a hundred feet or more high.

The Old Ones lie sleeping in the lost city of R'lyeh, waiting until the stars are right for their return. Time means noth-

ing to them, and humanity means even less. We are less to them
than the worms that crawl through the earth beneath our feet.

Read Up

Your best source for details about the Old Ones is, of
course, Lovecraft's original tales. If you don't have that
kind of time, though, check out The Encyclopedia Cthulhiana
by Daniel Harms or Ken Hite's Tarot of Cthulhu: Major Arcana,
a downloadable PDF you can use to foretell the future. Just be
careful not to play poker with these cards.

Play Up

"The Call of Cthulhu" is Lovecraft's best-known story, and
it's also the name of a tabletop roleplaying game (from Chao-
sium), a first-person computer game (from Headfirst Produc-
tions—plus a silent film (from the H.P. Lovecraft Historical
Society). To really immerse yourself in the madness, pick up
a Cthulhu game and start playing. Watch your SAN points drop
like people hurled from planes.

And if you understand what that means, then it's already
too late.

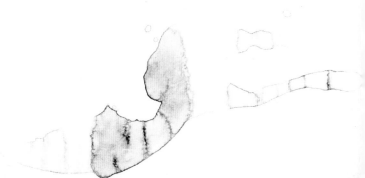

— 24. Use the Secret:

The Secret started out as a film that premiered in 2006, based on the ideas of Rhonda Byrne. Byrne later published a book that details the Secret, and on the back of endorsements from Oprah Winfrey, Larry King, and Ellen Degeneres, it's become a massive hit.

What Is the Secret?

The Secret is "the secret of life," or the best way to live a successful life. According to Byrne, her plan is based on the Law of Attraction. To sum up: Like attracts like.

Supposedly Byrne stumbled upon this ancient wisdom while reading a hundred-year-old book, *The Science of Getting Rich* by Wallace Wattles. The film shows interviews with many of the leading figures in the New Thought movement, from which the Secret springs.

How Do You Use It?

Since you can't control the world around you directly, you need to control what you can: yourself. In particular, your thoughts.

If you think positive thoughts, good things will happen to you. If you think negatively—for whatever reason—bad things will hound you.

The Secret, then, is to think good thoughts.

Is It That Simple?

Sure.

Er, not really.

In *The Secret*, you're told to "Ask, Believe, and Receive."

So, first you figure out what it is you really want. Then you believe in it. This is the tricky part, as you have to train or trick yourself to have that faith.

Then you have to be open to receiving what you want. The universe will supposedly show you signs to point you along the path toward getting what you want, as long as you're open and receptive to those signals.

Does It Work?

A lot of people certainly seem to think it does. A large number of skeptics point out, though, that these sort of ideas have been wandering around in popular thought for decades, mostly known as the power of positive thinking.

One thing for sure. It's worked extremely well for Rhonda Byrne.

25. Take Advantage of the Power of Prayer:

When many people are at the lowest points in their life, they turn to prayer for help. This has been the way since before recorded history. But does it really work? And if so, how can you best turn that to your advantage?

Do It Yourself

"There are no atheists in foxholes," or so the saying goes. Whether that's true or not, when you find yourself in dire straights with no other recourse, slap your hands together and start begging your favorite deity for your life. The worst it'll cost you is a few minutes of your time and perhaps the respect or your less-desperate friends.

When you petition God (or the gods, or whatever) for something, it's not necessary to try to strike a deal, but since you're (perhaps literally) under the gun, why not? Favorites include:

"I'll be good from now on."

"I'll go to church every Sunday."

"I'll enter a religious school and dedicate my life to your study and worship."

Of course, no one (including, perhaps, God) expects you to keep your end of the bargain. It's a deal made under duress, right?

Get Some Help

If one person praying can have some effect, then having lots should help even more, right?

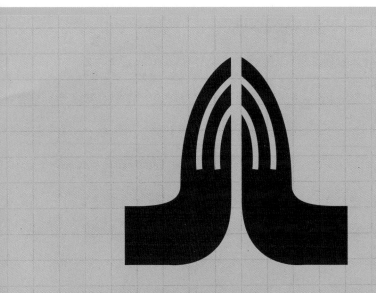

Maybe.

Scientists have debated this for over a century and conducted several studies in which people in hospitals were prayed for without their knowledge. Some of these have shown that the group that was prayed for did significantly better than the control group. Other studies have shown no difference between the two groups at all.

Of course, if you want people to pray for you, you're not going to have them do it in secret. Put out the word. Identify yourself. Ask for their prayers.

It may not work in any way that a double-blind experiment could measure, but it doesn't hurt to have all those people pulling for you either.

26. Use the Placebo Effect:

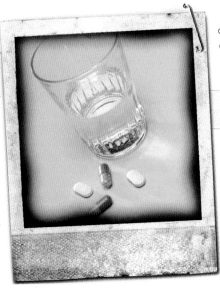

A placebo is a medicine or medical therapy that has no proven effect at all. In fact, it is proved to not work. But it does.

How a Placebo Works

The doctor (or parent, or whoever) gives the patient the placebo and tells her what it is supposed to do. The patient takes the medicine or undergoes the therapy, which has no direct effect on her. However, the power of suggestion makes her believe that she will become better, and so she does.

Making a Placebo Work

Unless you are extremely gullible, you cannot knowingly make a placebo work on yourself. It must be administered by some sort of authority figure, preferably a medical professional.

Some doctors even write out prescriptions for placebos and have the patients fill them at their local pharmacy. They even write "placebo" on the prescription pad so that the pharmacist knows to fill the bottle with sugar pills or something equally inert.

With the word "placebo" becoming better known all the time, other doctors have turned to using the word "obecalp" (placebo spelled backward) instead. If there's any confusion, the pharmacist can then call the doctor and get clearer instructions over the phone.

Placebos at Home

The next time somebody in your home complains of a headache or hangover, you could give the placebo effect a shot. Make a show of mixing something mysterious (say, sugar) in a glass of juice—or perhaps blending a bit of Sprite or 7-Up in with the juice—and then present it as your "Grandfather's No-Fail Headache Cure."

You may be surprised at the results. In any case, it'll give you some time to hunt down some ibuprofen for yourself.

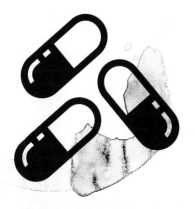

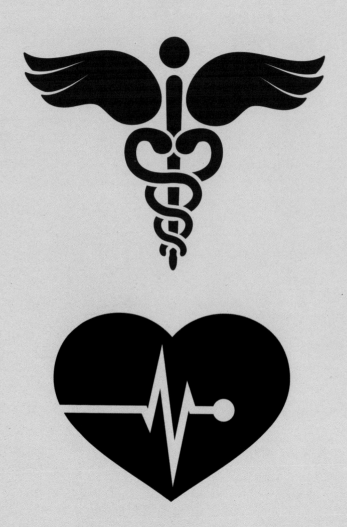

27. Talk Like a Pirate:

The popularity of films like *Pirates of the Caribbean* and the rise of International Talk Like a Pirate Day (September 19th) has made the emulation of long-gone murderers and thieves more fun than ever. You can strap on a cutlass, put a golden hoop in your ear, and slap a tricorn hat on your head, but even if you can strut your peg-legged walk while three sheets to the wind on grog, it doesn't matter if you can't talk the talk.

Pirate Vocabulary

Arrh: Gosh.

Ahoy: You there! Use this to get someone's attention. To make it clear who you're talking to, say, "Ahoy the" thing. To hail a ship called the Black Pearl, for example, you'd say, "Ahoy the Black Pearl!"

Avast: Hey! Attention!

Aye: Yes

Aye-Aye: Yes, sir.

Be: Are. As in "Be ye a sea monster?"

Booty: Treasure.

Grog: Water or weak beer and rum.

Hearty: Friend or shipmate.

Ho: Used with another word to indicate that you've seen it. For instance, if you spot a coast, you might say, "Land ho!"

Keelhaul: To punish someone by dragging them under the ship.

Lubber: Someone who does not sail.

Matey: A fellow sailor (a shipmate).

Me: My. As in "Shiver me timbers!"

Shanty: A sea song.

Ye: You.

Pirate Style

Most pirate talk has a distinct lilt to it that's closer to an Irish accent than anything else. A pirate sounds about as distant from a leprechaun as you can get though. He's gruff, mean, and snarls at everyone.

As a pirate, you are confident, surly, and sometimes lecherous to boot. The world is yours for the taking, and take it you will, one hapless ship at a time.

— 28. Swipe a Credit Card Number:

People worry about hackers stealing their credit card numbers online all the time. While there's certainly a risk of this, it's miniscule compared to the chance that some minimum-wage clerk will copy down the number off your card when you hand it to her after a good meal.

Skimming a Card

The easiest way to grab a credit card number that's not yours is to work in a restaurant, bar, or other business in which people routinely give you a card and let you walk away with it. While you're out of sight, all you have to do is copy down the card number, expiration date, and Card Security Code (the three or four numbers on the back of the card, near where it's signed).

If you're in a hurry, place a piece of paper over the credit card and rub it with a pencil or a crayon. This mimics the kind of impression that mechanical credit card machines used to take, long before the advent of the magnetic stripe all such cards now use. Just be sure to copy down the Card Security Code too.

Hacking for Numbers

If you're an international hacker, do your best to break into the customer database of a large retail site on the web. While they have the best security, making them the hardest to get into, they also have a treasure trove of credit card numbers for the taking.

If you can't pull that off, consider setting up a key capture program on a public computer instead, perhaps at your local college or at a nearby internet cafe. Once you grab the collected keystrokes, just look for a set of data that looks like credit card information, and you are good to go.

Don't Use It

Stealing someone's credit card information is a serious crime and carries stiff penalties. The best way to get caught is to go on a spending spree, max out the victim's card, and have everything shipped to your house.

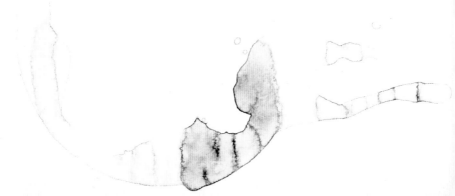

29. Buy and Sell Drugs:

In one sense, it's the American dream. See an opportunity and seize it. Find a market and satisfy it. Buy low and sell high.

The only trouble is that the market is illegal, and the product is deadly and ruins lives. But if you don't have a problem with that....

Buying Drugs

This is the easy part. There are dozens of people in any decent-sized city who would be happy to sell you drugs if you ask them. There are, of course, some catches. They could rob you, sell you bad drugs, beat you, kill you, and so on.

Most drug dealers won't bother with any of that though. They know the best way to get as much money out of you as possible is to make themselves your new best friend: your supplier. Then they can take you for every spare penny you have over the next several years of your life, until you either get clean or die.

If you're new to buying drugs, just ask around. Most times, the locals in an area know where drugs are being sold, even if they don't know the dealers personally.

Selling Drugs

Once you buy enough drugs, if you indulge in them, you'll find yourself addicted to them to some degree. Drugs do not come free, and the more you use them, the more money you blow on them. What better way to make money than to turn your addiction into a business?

Start out slow, selling drugs to your friends. Let the word spread from there.

Be careful not to step on the toes of your supplier. If he asks why you're suddenly buying so much more from him, be honest about it. He's going to find out anyhow, and the last thing you want to wind up in is a turf war. This is the perfect time to ask him for a volume discount.

30. Destroy a Political Opponent:

It doesn't take much to destroy a political hopeful these days. Here are ten quick tips.

1. Dig deep into his past. No one is without sin. Figure out what your foe's secrets are and then expose them to the world.

2. Portray him as weak. Find some issue on which your foe has been known to equivocate. Rather than recognize the complexity of the issue and respect the way he wrestles with it, announce that he is a lazy thinker who flip-flops on the issues because of a lack of convictions. Because people respect convictions far more than intellectual honesty.

3. Mock him. Catch him doing something silly, and mock it constantly. Turn on *The Daily Show* if you run shy of any ideas for this. It's chock full of mockeriffic notions.

4. Lie about him. Distort your opponent's record any chance you get. Make him sound like the bill he sponsored about saving babies actually offered them up to butchers as free meat.

5. Divide his team. Dig into the past of his political team. If you find anything remotely questionable in any one of their backgrounds, question not only that person's past but your foe's judgment for having anything to do with them.

6. Attack his family. Dig into the lives of his spouse and kids. Claim any problems they have show his moral deficiency and that of the people around him.

7. Attack his friends. If the candidate ever talked with anyone with a shady past, point out how this shows his recklessness.

8. Frame him for a crime. Laugh privately when he claims it's a set-up and ask him if he actually saw the one-armed man who really did it.

9. Have him followed. Maybe you'll find him in the arms of a young person who is not his spouse.

10. Play the victim. Anytime he says anything to you, much less against you, feign disgust at the way he panders to everyone around him.

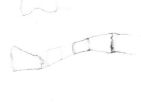
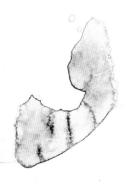

31. Play with Booze and Fire:

Pure alcohol burns so well that we can use it as an alternative fuel to gasoline for cars. This means you can have all sorts of fun with the less pure stuff that you can find in any well-stocked bar.

Get Proof

To get a decent flame from a drink, it should be at least 100 proof (50% alcohol). The higher the alcohol content, the easier it is for a liquid to burn. Those who regularly mess around with drinks and lighters usually employ Everclear (190 proof) or Barcardi 151 (151 proof).

Because of their high alcohol content, these drinks normally come mixed with something else to make them more palatable. When working with fire, though, it's best to stick to plain liquor straight up.

Play with Fire

Next, find yourself a decent source of fire. You can use a lighter, but turning the thing upside-down to get the flame nearer to the booze can cause you to set your thumb on fire.

Instead, get one of those long-tipped butane lighters used for lighting barbecue grills. In a pinch, a match works well too, as long as you work quickly. Just don't forget to put the match out when you're done with it.

Favorite Flames

The most popular mixture of booze and fire is the flaming shot. To pull this off:

1. **Get a high-proof shot.**

2. **Light it.**

3. **Slam it.**

4. **Close your mouth.**

If you do this right, the fire will burn out shortly after entering your mouth, as closing your mouth suffocates the blaze. Of course, if you blow it, just remember those famous words every kid learns during the fire safety classes at school. "Stop, drop, and roll."

And Liberty for All

The Statue of Liberty is a fun variant on the standard flaming shot. To handle this one:

1. Get a shot.

2. Dip your finger in it.

3. Have a friend light your finger.

4. Hold your finger up like a torch as you slam back the shot.

5. Stick your finger in your mouth and close it to extinguish the flame.

32. Become an E-Mail Spammer:

You see the messages in your e-mail inbox every day. Buy viagra cheap! Enlarge your penis! Help out a Nigerian billionaire in dire straights! Buy this penny stock cheap!

Spam like this entices gullible people who don't know any better to part with their hard-earned cash. They sell items that would not be allowed in any store—not because they're illegal, but instead useless.

So how can you get in on that?

Collect Addresses

First you need to have e-mail addresses to which you can send your spam. You can purchase this from a list merchant or start collating a list on your own. Since e-mail costs you nothing but a little server time, gather as many as you possibly can, and don't worry if most of them don't work anyhow. You're not going to leave your e-mail addresses up long enough to worry about the bounce back messages.

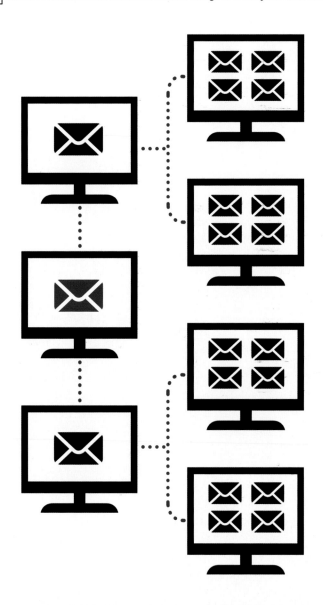

Find a Compliant ISP

Most legitimate internet service providers (ISPs) have policies and programs in place to put a stop to spammers. If you try to send out too many messages at once, they stop you cold and may even terminate your account.

Some ISPs aren't so civic minded though and are happy to take your business no matter what your plans may be.

Construct Your E-Mail

Figure out what it is you're selling. There's no point in spamming people just for fun. Maybe you have shoddy or gray-market goods you want to move. Perhaps you're after the referral fees that legitimate businesses offer up to people who send customers to their websites.

Most e-mail accounts use filters to kill off spam before the recipient even sees them. You can get around this by altering your text slightly so that a person can read it but a spam-killing program lets its pass by. By spelling the name of your favorite erectile disfunction drug as V!agra, for instance, you can slip your message past many filters.

Spamware

If you're too lazy to do all this yourself, you can purchase spamware packages to help you out. This kind of software is currently illegal in eight states, so check your local laws first. Then you can start sending out your spam right away— probably trying to sell spamware to other unscrupulous folks like yourself.

33. Run a Nigerian E-Mail Scam:

If you own an e-mail account, you've probably received dozens of letters from countries you've barely heard of in which the writer asks for your help in moving a large amount of cash out of his country. If you're smart, you just trashed these notes or flagged them as spam. If you fell for them, then write in to us and ask about opportunities with this publisher as well.

Advance Fees and Other Lies

This sort of e-mail is the opening gambit in an advance fee fraud. In it, you state that you know of the existence of a large amount of secret cash but you cannot get to it directly. For that, you need help in perpe-trating a fraud, by having your mark posing as someone who has the right to the money so that he can gain access to it. In exchange, you promise him a cut of the millions you stand to make.

So far, this sounds great to the recipient. He gets wealth beyond his wildest dreams, and all he has to do is lie to some officials in a distant land. Most people know that this is too good to be true, but some sign up for it and start planning what to do with all that cash.

When you send out a million spam e-mails at a time with this sort of fraud, all you need is one person to fall for it and sign on.

Just a Little Help, Please

Once you have a mark on the hook, provide your new friend with all sorts of forged "proof" of the legitimacy of your claims. With the promise of easy money from gullible people, you may even be able to get a legitimate government official to help you out. If possible, you should use stolen identities of innocent and ignorant locals instead of your own. You don't want this traced back to you when it inevitably goes wrong.

Then send your new best friend a message. "We need a thousand dollars to bribe an official." Or "We need to have at least $100,000 in a local bank account to be able to take delivery of the money." End with, "Given the large amount of money we stand to make, can you help out with this small favor?"

Start out low and ramp the fees up as you go. The more money the mark puts into this deal, the more obliged he will feel to keep throwing good money after what he's already sent. He

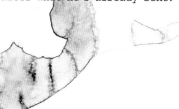

might even start raiding his retirement account, borrowing from his friends and family, or even embezzling from his boss in the hopes that he'll be able to pay it all back before anyone notices.

Of course, you never send out a dime. Eventually the mark will figure this out, or someone will clue him in, but until then you can keep milking him for every cent he and everyone he knows has.

34. Knock Someone Out:

You see it on every cheesy detective show in the world. The PI walks into a room and a shadowy figure steps up and pistol whips him from behind. The detective slumps over unconscious but otherwise unharmed. He wakes up a short time later with blood all over the place and a still-hot pistol in his hand. He's been framed for a murder and it all goes downhill from there.

Reality Check

In real life, it doesn't work this way. When someone loses consciousness from a blow, it almost always means he's sustained a serious concussion. When the victim wakes up, he will be hurt and disoriented and may vomit.

That's not the worst-case scenario. A hit that can knock someone out might kill them instead. It's easy to see how a blow to the skull might crack it wide open or how a severe concussion could lead to bleeding in the brain.

In other words, don't try this at home.

Hit Fast and Hard

If you need to knock someone out, there are two simple ways to do it: punching or choking. Again, either can be lethal, so attempt these only as a last resort. It's often enough to hit someone hard and then run away while they're hurting. Knocking them out isn't necessary.

Knock-Out Punch

Swing your fist hard and fast straight at the center of your target's jaw. Aim right through him rather than trying to jab. With a solid enough hit, you will slam his head back fast enough to rattle his brain, which is what you're hoping to do. You might break your hand doing this, but if you're that desperate it may be a small price to pay.

The Dim Mak school of martial arts—which focuses on the delivery of strikes to bundles of nerves in the victim's body—prescribes striking your foe in the temple with a shaped fist. This, again, can be lethal.

Choke-Out

On either side of the throat, there's a carotid artery. You can feel your pulse in it with your bare fingers. Pressure on these cuts off circulation of blood to the brain, which eventually causes the victim to pass out. This doesn't carry the risk of head trauma, but it can kill if you keep the pressure up for too long. Again, it's better to hit and run.

35. Steal a Password/PIN:

In our modern economy, we use passwords and PINs (Personal Information Numbers) to guard much of our financial data. If you can get a hold of someone else's password, it's like having a key to their wallet. Getting them isn't easy, but it can be done.

Spying

The simplest way to steal a password or PIN is to watch the person as they use it. You can peer over the victim's shoulder in a store checkout line or at an ATM. Then all you have to do is steal the debit card and use it freely—at least until the loss is reported.

If you have more control over the area, you can be a bit more subtle. Use a pair of high-powered binoculars to watch someone at an ATM across the street. Mount a wireless video camera behind someone sitting at a computer and record their actions so you can then rewind and copy down their account informaion.

Key-Capture Programs

Find a program that captures keystrokes and then install it on a public computer. Some viruses can do this for you—if you're a hacker and know how to deploy them—but if you have physical access to a computer you can do this yourself.

Once you have the program installed, it copies down every keystroke, including any account names and passwords. You just have to go back through the logs to find them.

36. Screw Up Someone's Computer:

Computers are delicate machines, and even when they're working well they can crash. It sometimes seems like it's a miracle they ever manage to boot up at all.

It's not too hard, then, to give a computer the nudge it needs to tip it right over the edge into oblivion. There are two different tactics: physical and electronic.

Physical Damage

Computers don't like water, heat, or dirt.

If the computer you wish to damage is a laptop, pour a bit of water into the keyboard or give it a quick dip in a filled bathtub or sink. Then turn it on. If it dries out before you can activate it, it might not be damaged right away, but water damage can cause corrosion that will harm the computer days, weeks, or even months later.

To cause a computer to heat up, just block the air vents on it. A few strips of packing tape over these can make the temperature spike in a short while. This works especially well if the computer is under a desk where no one usually looks at it.

Alternatively, you can stick a paperclip through the exhaust and jam the blades of the fan.

To gunk up the mechanisms in the computer and cause other heat problems, take a bit of baby powder or some other fine, dust-like material, and blow it into the machine. This may take a little longer to work than the other methods, but that means you can be long gone when it starts to fry.

Or just take a hammer to the damned thing.

Electronic Damage

If you have access to a machine, it's easy to cause trouble. You can just go in and delete important files or move things about and rename them so they're harder to find.

To be more subtle about it, just turn off the machine's virus protection and lower the computer's firewall. Then let the internet screw up the machine for you.

Word to the Wise

If this all gives you pause, back up your own machine regularly. It doesn't take malicious action for you to lose everything.

37. Live In Your Car:

With the ongoing housing crisis in full swing, more and more people are becoming homeless all the time. If you find yourself without a place to live, there's always one other place you can turn: your car.

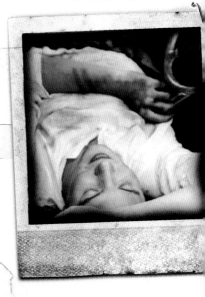

The Right Place

Sleeping in your car is easy. Just put the seat back and relax. If you're fortunate enough to have a van, you might even have enough room to lay down a proper mattress in the back. The trick is finding a place to put your car where it's both safe and unlikely to draw attention.

Some interstate rest stops encourage people to stop and rest for a few hours at night. Truck stops are full of idle trucks in which the drivers sleep at night, and no one bothers them a bit. A smaller car might stand out here, but it's worth a shot.

Getting privacy in a regular sedan can be tricky. If you still have spare bedsheets, you can use them to cover up the windows from the inside. This blocks out both glaring lights and prying eyes. Cardboard cut to the right dimensions is cheap and works well too.

Safety First

Be sure to lock your doors if you're in a questionable neighborhood, and leave your keys in the ignition if you think you might need to make a quick escape. Always have enough gas in the car to get at least a few miles away, preferably to the next gas station at least.

Be careful not to run down the car's battery. While it's tempting to keep the lights on well after dark, you don't want to have to stop to ask someone for jumper cables and a bit of juice when you're in a hurry. If you can manage it, stick with flashlights instead. Keep one for general use and a little one for an emergency backup.

If you can afford the gas, start the car up and take it for a drive every few days. This helps recharge the battery and get rid of the crud that can build up in an engine from lack of use.

Keep Clean

Clean out your car regularly. When you're living in a small place, it's easy for it to get filthy. You won't be able to cook, and take-out wrappers and leftovers can draw bugs and other vermin quickly.

Find a way to get yourself clean too. A public restroom works in a pinch, or you can see if you can get a day pass to a local health club or Y. Keeping yourself in order helps stave off depression and makes it more likely you'll be able to land the kind of job you need to get you out of your wheels and into a less mobile home.

38. Amputate a Limb:

It's one of the most horrific things to think about—losing a part of your own body—but it's better to cut loose a piece if it means a chance to save your life. Some people have even managed to do this to themselves when necessary.

This is of course a last resort, often only employed if a part of the body is trapped and unable to be freed. Perhaps it's caught in a burning thresher or crushed under a boulder, leaving the victim no other way to get free and to help. However, an impromptu amputation in the field is likely to kill you too. Only try this if the alternative is clearly death.

Here's how to do it.

Make a Tourniquet

If you haven't already done so, make a tourniquet and place it around the limb that's about to be lost. This will help deaden the pain of the cutting and also prevent you from bleeding out after the loss of the limb. Place the tourniquet as far down the limb as you can manage so that you can save as much flesh as possible.

Use a Sharp Knife

The sharper the blade you can find, the better. Dull knives hurt more and can slip during the procedure.

Find a Space in the Bones—or Make One

The hardest part of any amputation is getting through the bone. If you have a saw handy, you may be able to cut right through the bone. Otherwise, you may be forced to break it. Place the bone on something firm and use your weight as leverage to snap it.

If this isn't possible, look for the nearest joint to the damaged area. It's far easier to cut through cartilage and tendons than through solid bone.

Get Medical Help

Once you're free, administer what first aid you can to stop the bleeding and help with the shock. Then get proper medical attention right away. With luck, you'll live.

39. Try Team Card Counting :

Counting cards while playing blackjack isn't illegal, but it's frowned upon. While the technique is beyond the casual player, serious gamblers know that it's the one sure-fire way to gain the necessary edge to make yourself a winner rather than a loser.

Working Alone

In the easiest card counting system (and there are many), you keep a running total of the relative value of the cards that have already been played. In this way, you can tell when the deck is rich in cards that work in the player's (your) favor.

The standard Hi-Lo system is the easiest. Cards 2 through 6 add +1 to the count, and cards 10 through Ace take –1. The other cards you ignore.

When the count is high, you raise your bet. The higher the count, the more you raise it. You do the reverse when the count is low.

The trouble is that it's easy to spot your betting pattern if you use this system. When a casino sees this, they'll ask you to leave. Then they'll tell you.

Teams Work

The famous MIT card-counting teams worked up a slick solution to this problem. It only takes two people, but more are even better.

A counter sits at the table and plays. He keeps his bets small and never varies them, but he keeps track of the count. When it gets high, he gives a secret signal to his partner, the bettor.

The bettor then rolls in, lays down a huge pile of cash, and starts making large bets. When the count falls lower, she gathers her chips and walks away—hopefully to another table where another card-counting parter has a hot card shoe waiting for her.

Variety Works Too

The casinos know all about this strategy now. You might be able to get away with it for a while, but eventually they'll catch on and ban you from their place. Then they'll put your face on a registry that will get you banned from every other major casino too.

40. Do a Keg Stand:

Most drinking games have to do with playing cards, dice, or even hand signals. The venerable keg stand, though, involves a bit of strength, balance, and intestinal fortitude. For all that, it's a simple contest.

Required Items

For a keg stand contest you need:

1. A keg of beer. A full half-barrel works best, especially the ones with cut-out handles on the top rim. Smaller ones can tip, and even a half-barrel can topple if there's not enough beer left in it.

2. A willing player. It's best to try this before you've had too much to drink. Getting turned upside down can have unfortunate effects on the digestive system of those with too much already in their bellies.

3. A tipping and spotting team. A single strong person can play this role, but keg stands are best when performed with a crowd, so get at least two or three people if you can.

4. A tapper. Someone needs to handle the tap for the brave keg-stander.

Performing a Keg Stand

This is a simple process. Just don't drop the drinker.

1. The keg-stander grabs the top of the keg and braces himself.

2. The tippers grab his legs and turn him upside-down so that he's doing a handstand atop the keg. If you can spare a few people as spotters, they can stand nearby and catch the keg-stander if anyone slips.

3. The tapper puts the tap into the keg-stander's mouth and opens it.

4. The keg-stander drinks for as long as he can. The crowd chants out the seconds as they roll by.

5. When the keg-stander has had enough, he shakes his head or pulls his mouth off of the tap. The tapper closes the tap, and the tippers lower the keg-stander back to the ground.

6. Everyone cheers.

Once this is over, others can try to break the keg-stander's time record. This can go on until there are no more challengers—or they run out of beer.

41. Build and Use a Beer Bong:

A beer bong is a homemade device designed to get the most beer into a drinker in the shortest amount of time possible. It's a simple device that young people have used to stupefy themselves with for decades.

Building the Beer Bong

To build a beer bong, you need three things, all of which you should be able to find in any hardware store:

1. A funnel. The larger, the better.

2. A length of plastic tubing cut about as long as your arm. The tubing should be just wide enough to fit around the end of the funnel.

3. A circular clamp. You can do without this if necessary, but you risk losing beer if it all comes apart.

Putting the beer bong together is easy. Just put the clamp around one end of the tube. Then jam the end of the funnel into that end of the tube. Tighten the clamp, and you're done.

Using the Beer Bong

Here's the fun part—if you like this sort of thing.

Fill the beer bong with beer. Anything stronger will likely send the drinker into a coma.

When filling the beer bong, hold it so that both ends are roughly level with the tubing curling down between them. Once it's full, place your thumb over the open end of the tube and pull that end of the device down. This lets the extra air out of the beer bong.

When you're ready, bring the beer bong to your mouth and stuff it in with one hand. Raise the funnel with your other hand.

Gravity and the lack of any resisting air pressure lets the beer slide right into as if you'd poured it over a waterfall. Swallow as fast as you can. If you fail, try to stuff your thumb back over the end of the tubing or you'll end up wearing the rest of it.

If you get it all down, holler about your studliness and then stagger off into a corner to collapse. Make sure your friends keep an eye on you, just in case.

Warning

It's easy to overdo it with a beer bong. Be cautious of the signs of alcohol poisoning. Also, those who have done a beer bong have been known to regurgitate the beer as quickly as they ingested it. This is a practice best handled outside.

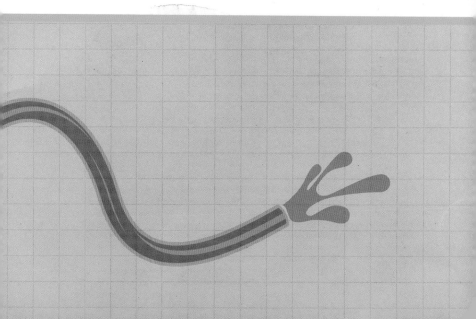

42. Jump from an Airplane:

Some people do it for sport. Others do it for their country. A sad few do it out of desperation. In each case, they're doing something unnatural: leaping out of an (often perfectly good) airplane.

Grab a Parachute

Despite what you may have seen in a James Bond movie, if you leave the aircraft without a working parachute, you are going to die. The chances of you being able to dive through the air and catch up to someone with a working parachute, steal his chute, and then successfully get away are zero.

Get Out

If you manage to get yourself strapped in properly and you know what you're doing, you have an excellent chance of surviving. Only about 1 in 100,000 jumps in the US prove fatal each year.

Of course, that assumes you know what you're doing.

Arch Your Back

Throw your arms and legs back to form a giant X and arch
your back. In this formation, you should be able to stabilize
yourself. You need to do this before you release your chute.
If you're spinning around like a top when your chute opens up,
you're going to get wrapped up in it. A chute that's wrapped
around you instead of the air above you works more like a
blanket than a parachute.

Grab Your Ripcord

Once you're stable, grab your ripcord. It should be brightly
colored and located someplace on your chest. It often looks
like a shiny ring. Brace yourself, and pull it.

Once your chute deploys, look for a couple of loops attached
to your shoulders. These control the steering mechanism for
the chute. Play with them a bit and get a feel for them, but
don't pull too hard.

If you see a pair of steel circles on your shoulders, don't
pull those until you're on the ground. Those release your
chute, which is fine when you're standing on terra firma but not
so great a thousand feet up.

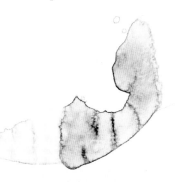
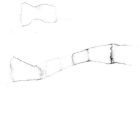

Tuck and Roll

If you're trained well and time it just right, you can pull off one of those fancy landings in which you tiptoe onto the ground. If you blow it, though, you'll break your legs. Better to not try it and just go with the old standby: tuck and roll.

Put your feet tight together and bend your knees just a bit. When you hit the ground, let your knees tuck toward you and then roll forward and to the side. This lets you safely absorb your momentum rather than blowing out your knees.

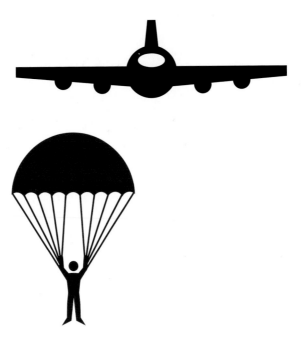

43. Practice Gun Fu:

If you've watched too many John Woo movies, you know that all true gunsels hold their pistols sideways and out away from their bodies as they empty clip after clip into their foes. It's ridiculous, and it makes it hard to hit anything you think you might be aiming at, but it looks cool.

So, if style means more to you than actually hitting anything with a bullet, then gun fu is for you.

Shoot Wild but Pretty

Use semi-automatic pistols or at least learn how to pull that trigger fast. Gun fu practitioners buy bullets in bulk and throw them around like a flower girl tosses petals.

It doesn't matter if you hit your target, at least not right away. You can chase them down with bullets, herd them into the place you want them to be, and then administer a balletic coup de grace that will make your victim appreciate how beautifully you stole his final breath.

Use as Many Guns as You Can

Put a machine-pistol in each hand, an assault rifle slung across your back, and a sawed-off shotgun on your hip. Use them in tandem and individually in any order you can manage. Bonus points for establishing some kind of beat. Double that if you can dance to it.

Ammo like Water

Run through enough ammunition that you'll need to carry your spare clips in a cart you pull behind you—between scenes in the movie that is your life, of course. In the heat of battle, drop magazines out of your weapons one-handed, letting them fall to the ground. Then flip spare clips out of your sleeves and straight into the guns once again.

Cock your weapons with one hand, especially shotguns. That way you can fill both of your fists with them at once.

Die a Blood Death

Unless you're the hero of this flick, be prepared to die by the weapon of your choice. You should have spent all that practice time playing mah jong instead for all the good it will do you.

44. Get Hit by a Car and Survive:

Do yourself a favor and do like your momma taught you. Look both ways before you cross the street, and don't play in traffic. You'll live a lot longer that way.

If you still find yourself on the wrong side of a fast-moving grill, let's hope the words in this chapter find enough time to flash through your head before you die. Then you can at least tell St. Peter you gave it a shot.

Watch the Road

If you see the car coming, you may have a chance. Figure out which way it's going and dive in the other direction. Just try not to dive into more traffic if you can.

Seek Cover

If this is no accident—if someone's actually trying to hit you with the car—then dive behind something solid. All but the most determined hit-and-run artists won't purposely destroy their car trying to get at you. After all, if they crack up the car, they blow that ever-important "run" part of their plan.

Up and Over

If you cannot get away from the car, for whatever reason, then jump up. Get as high as you can, and pull your legs up after you. If you're channeling Michael Jordan—or facing a really short car—you might even be able to clear the top of the vehicle and let it pass under. Chances are, though, that you'll get at least clipped instead.

Still, bouncing off the top of a car beats having it run over you any day.

Roll with It

Once you've been hit, pull yourself into a ball and cover up your head with your arms if you can. The impact is likely to send you flying, and the better your landing, the better your chance of surviving. If you flail about trying to flap away through the air, you're only going to break a limb or—worse—your neck.

45. Avoid Ebola:

Ebola is one of the most destructive viruses on the planet, with a fatality rate of anywhere from 50-90%, depending on the strain you happen to contract. No vaccines have been approved for use against it, and there is no known cure.

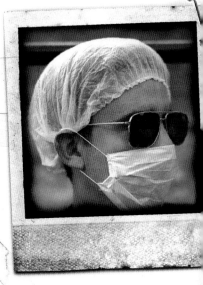

Stay Out of Africa

The ebola virus harms not only humans but lower forms of primates in the wild too. Most of the outbreaks have happened in Africa, often starting with people handing monkeys or gorillas or even antelopes. It then moves among the human population via contact with infected blood or bodily fluids. It can also be transmitted via medical equipment like needles or scalpels that have been used on infected patients and then properly cleaned.

Recognize the Symptoms

Ebola symptoms can vary a lot, making it hard to identify quickly. They can start with fever, dizziness, headaches, joint or muscle pain, weakness, nausea, and more. In later stages, the patient can suffer from red eyes, vomiting blood, bloody diarrhea, and various hemorrhages.

If you have such symptoms, get to a decent hospital as fast as you can. It's your best chance to survive and—failing that—not infect those around you. Ebola can be detected by lab tests on urine and saliva. If it's found in you, be prepared to spend the next week in a very tight and protected environment. If you live more than two weeks, you should be good, as few if any make it beyond that.

For the Future

Scientists have formulated successful vaccines for monkeys, but none have worked in human trials yet. Also, once those vaccines are discovered, they still will have to be administered within the first four days after symptoms start, or it will already be too late.

46. Curse Effectively:

It's easy to cuss. Anyone can do it. Just try it in front of a four-year-old and then watch how well she can mimic you—in front of her parents.

Be Creative

Any idiot can drop the F-bomb. In many circles, it's as common as using a comma. Telling someone "Fuck off" won't faze them a bit. To really offend someone, you need to bring your A-game to the table.

Try something like, "Fuck me gently with a chainsaw." The imagery is both gross and effective. It grabs your attention and refuses to let go.

Variety Is Your Friend

Believe it or not, if you say, "Fuck me gently with a chain-saw" often enough, you might as well just say "Hello." People around you will start to expect it, and when they hear it, they'll just roll their eyes.

This is nothing new. It's not offensive. It's droll.

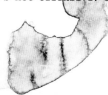

To keep offending people, you need to come up with new things. It's not enough to spit out variations on themes you've already blunted by grinding them too hard. You need to some up with something entirely new.

Circumstances Change

Truly gifted cursers come up with new curses on the fly, based on the situation at hand. If you're at a basketball game and the ref makes a bad call, try riffing on how he can take his needle-dick and fuck the airhole in the ball. If you're watching a horse race, you could comment on how the jockey's mother could ride him home better than he's riding the horse.

. The key is coming up with new ways to offend, but as long as the world keeps giving you new situations, this is a challenge you can overcome.

F#@K OFF

47. Make a Deathbed Conversion:

You might have been an atheist your whole life. Perhaps you laugh pityingly at the people who head to church every week and who tithe ten percent of their pre-tax earnings to the support of their chosen religion. But when you're expecting a visit from the Grim Reaper any minute now, preparing yourself for the afterlife might not seem too pointless.

It's Not Too Late

As long as you're alive and conscious, it's not too late to change your mind—in some traditions. A number of clergy consider it cheating to plea for mercy at the last second after living a life filled with wickedness. Others happily accept the possibility that you can do such a thing, but only if you truly believe.

Who's to judge that? Why, God, of course, and if you think you can fool Him, then there's a good chance your conversion isn't quite complete.

It's All in the Timing

The trick for a good deathbed conversion is to make sure you have the time to complete it. If you die in an airplane crash, you may have time to convert on the way down, but if you're killed in a car crash or by a stray bullet, you may not have the time to have any such thoughts pass through your head.

48. Find a G-Spot:

If you want to make your girl-friend or wife very happy, go out of your way to find their G-spot. Named after Ernst Gräfenberg, the German gynecologist who first publicized the idea of such a spot, the G-spot is a special area inside of a woman's vagina. If you can find it and properly stimulate it, you can drive her to the most powerful orgasms she's ever had.

Then she's sure to make you her new best friend.

Where Is It?

The G-spot is supposedly located along the front of the vaginal wall. However, no scientific research has been able to establish this for sure. Still, it's fun to look for it, so keep trying.

Female Ejaculation

Some claim that proper stimulation of the G-spot leads to such strong orgasms that they can cause a woman to ejaculate from her vagina a clear fluid that is plainly not urine. While even the existence of this fluid was long a subject of debate, research has shown that it does exist.

Many (but not all) women have a special organ called the Skene's glands, and it's from here that the fluid comes. Whether or not this is the source of the G-spot, though, is still up for debate.

Break Out the Ultrasound

Researchers in Britain claim to be able to determine if a woman has a G-spot or not by the use of an ultrasound machine. If the front wall of the woman's vagina has an area of thicker tissue—what these scientists have defined as the G-spot—then the woman can have vaginal (as opposed to clitoral) orgasms.

So if you can't find it on your own, a simple test may some-day be able to determine if there's one to be found in any particular woman at all.

49. Work as a Drug Mule:

The smuggling of drugs is a dangerous but lucrative occupation. It's become so profitable that some people are willing to directly risk their lives in exchange for the money they can earn.

Muling Up

To be a drug mule, you must swallow a number of small, drug-packed latex balloons shortly before boarding a flight. These are usually either condoms or the fingers of surgical gloves, and they are often lubricated to make them easier to ingest.

The Dangers of Muling

The drugs of choice are high-grade heroin or cocaine. If any one of the balloons burst while inside of you, the amount of drugs that will flow straight into your body is enough to overdose and kill you. This can happen for any number of reasons, which is what makes working as a drug mule so dangerous—other than the real risk of being caught.

Muling Out

Once you get to your destination, you take some strong laxatives and then get to work removing the drugs from your body the hard way. You want to get the balloons out as fast as possible to reduce the chance that your stomach acids might finally eat through any one of them and kill you. You then fish the goods out of the toilet, deliver them to your contact in the new country, and collect your cash.

Getting Caught

Your troubles can really start if customs officials decide that you seem like a mule. While in many countries they cannot X-ray you to detect the balloons or force-feed you laxatives to get them to come out, they can hold you for a certain period of time and wait. Eventually, you'll have to move your bowels, and the drugs will come out.

Of course, the longer you try to hold the balloons in your body, the better the chance that one of them might burst inside of you. This is not the kind of waiting game in which you really want to be involved.

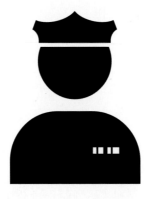

50. Work as a Coyote:

A coyote is a term used for smugglers who specialize in getting people across borders illegally. The skills of such smugglers are in high demand around the world, although they are most famous for their work along the US-Mexico border.

Finding Clients

Once you establish a reputation as a coyote, you don't often have to go looking for clients. People will seek you out instead. You just need to make yourself and your successes know.

Many coyotes work as part of a team. While the real coyotes are those who take the risk of getting people across the border, they also may have agents who help make arrangements with their clients for them. Some of these agents have been around for years. When one coyote or group of coyotes is arrested, they simply find new people to take their place.

Getting Across

Crossing a guarded border with a group of people is no mean feat. To pull it off, the coyote must have some kind of plan. Perhaps he knows a border guard he can bribe. Or he might have dug a tunnel through which he can lead his clients. Or maybe he just knows the borderlands better than anyone else and can lead his people safely through a land in which they might otherwise die.

Getting More Work

Don't be tempted to let your clients die, even if it might save you from jail. There's nothing to get the border guards up like finding a truckload of people who suffocated to death in the back of a truck because their coyote abandoned them there rather than risk facing the law. Even if you get away, remember that these people have families, possibly on both sides of the border, and families have a penchant for taking revenge.

Do well by your clients, and you will get their business again and again. Many people like to be able to visit their homeland once in a while, and if they think they can depend on you to get them back across again safely, they're bound to return more often—and pay you a new fee each time.

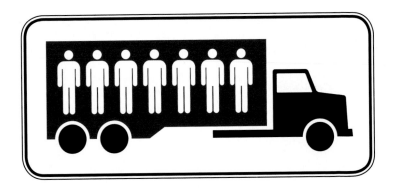

51. Enter a Country Illegally:

All sorts of people would like to be able to move about the world freely if they could. Unfortunately, we have border guards and customs officials enforcing the laws that bar their way.

The Easy Way

Get yourself a passport and go to the other country. Once you're there, stay. Immigration officials might come looking for you at your last reported address, but if you're smart you won't be there when they pop around.

The trick, of course, is that you have to then live off the books. You cannot have a bank account or purchase anything that would require you to show identification. Also, you cannot leave the country. If you do and try to re-enter later, you're bound to have a hard time of it.

Still, you can satisfy the visa requirements of many countries by simply leaving and coming back on a regular basis. Just keep track of the local laws, and you're all set.

– The Hard Way –

If you have money, you can hire a coyote (see the previous entry) or some other professional to smuggle you across the border. While this costs money, it can be well spent if it keeps you from dying in the desert.

If that's not an option, look for other people trying to cross the border illegally and then follow them. If you can, make friends with them and cross the border as a team. You don't want them thinking you're the law trying to follow them and then arrest them. Some folks get violent about that kind of misunderstanding.

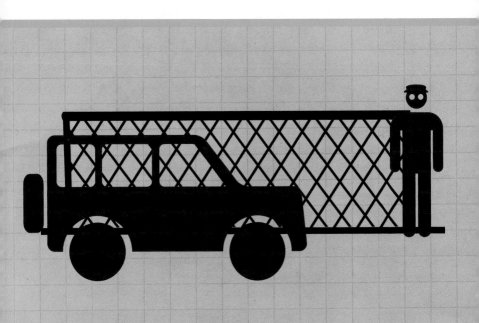

52. Write a Fake Memoir:

Just follow this step-by-step process to come up with your best-selling memoir—that will eventually be exposed as a pack of lies.

1. Have yourself a life.

2. Write about it.

3. Realize it's damned dull.

4. Figure out what would spice it up.

5. Don't bother to actually do those things, as that would involve:
   a. Work.
   b. Risk.
   c. Trouble.
   d. A huge mess.
   e. All of the above.

6. Write about how your life should have been, had certain things that could have happened happened and how you'd have reacted to them in a way that you would like to think you would.

7. Show this to a literary agent who specializes in spicy, true-life tales.

8. Go back and create proof of the fake elements in your life while you wait for the results of the rights auction.

9. Cash the check, appear on *Oprah*, and laugh all the way to the bank.

10. Be found out, issue a heartfelt confession, plead for forgiveness. Then lay low for a year or two before coming back with a new book. This time, call it a novel.

53. Get Your Fake Memoir Published:

Once you've finished your master-
piece of "literary nonfiction," it's
time to figure out how to get it in
front of the reading public so that
people everywhere can recognize your
genius at fabricating what an incred-
ible life you've led.

Find an Agent

It used to be that the editors
at the big publishing houses went
through the stack of manuscript prospective authors sent to them, search-
ing for something to fall in love
with and publish. With the advent of
computers making it easier for anyone
to try to write, weeding through this
"slush pile" became like hunting for a needle in a haystack.

For this reason, most publishers only look at manuscripts
shown to them by literary agents these days. They don't buy
everything they see, but the process cuts way down on the
amount of work they have to do to find a worthy manuscript.

Agents work their way through their own slush piles instead,
and when they find a good prospect, they use their knowledge
of and contacts in the book publishing industry to find the

best editors and publishers for the book. With the talent you've shown in concocting great stories about yourself, you shouldn't have any problem pulling the wool over the eyes of an agent weary with reading about people who are honestly far duller.

Be a Wary Writer

While there are many excellent agents out there, a reputable agent will never ask for money from you. They take roughly 15% of any money they make for you by selling your book to a publisher, but they do not get any cash from you up front.

If an agent asks you for a reading fee or money with which to pay an editor to clean up your book, run screaming for the hills. They are likely preying on your dreams of becoming published to milk you for every dime they can get.

For evaluations of various agents, be sure to check out websites like Preditors & Editors (*http://anotherealm.com/pre-deditors*) or Writer Beware (*www.sfwa.org/beware*).

Keep Fabricating

The process of an agent submitting a book can take a long time. Be patient. Don't bug your agent too often, much as you'll want hourly updates. And keep fabricating your "life story."

It's easy to hold your breath and not do anything while you wait for the offers for your book to start rolling in. To keep your mind off such obsessive thoughts, start work on the next volume of your fake memoir instead. That way you'll be ready, when an editor says, "We love it. Do you have anything you could add for a sequel too?"

54. Self-Publish Your Fake Memoir:

If you can string words together to make sentences, you have what it takes to get published, especially if you can spice them up with fantastic tales aggrandizing your life. The advent of desktop publishing means that anyone with a computer is only a few steps away from becoming a published author, and that includes you!

Write Something

You can't publish words that don't exist. Sit down in front of a computer and start typing. Find something you know about—or come up with a story you want to tell, like about how you battled your drug addiction while touring with the Grateful Dead through Afghanistan on a secret mission for the Navy SEALs—and then write, write, write.

The trick with writing anything is to stick with it until you finish. Many more books get started than completed. Don't stop to revise every sentence. That's what a second draft is for. Plow through until the end and then go back and change things later.

Oh, and make sure the lies all line up.

Find a Printer

It used to be that printing a book was an expensive proposition because you needed to be able to pony up the money to print thousands of copies to be able to bring the price down to a reasonable level. Today, with print-on-demand (POD) technology, you can print as few as a single copy at a time.

Print-on-demand books don't quite have the quality of traditionally printed books. These are essentially laser-printed pages bound under a cover made by using a color laser-printer on thick cardstock. However, as the technology improves, so does the appearance of the books.

The most popular print-on-demand services are Lightning Source (a division of giant book distributor Ingram), BookSurge (a division of *Amazon.com*), and *Lulu.com*.

Start Selling

Once you have your books, it's time to start selling them. This can be as challenging as actually writing the book, which is a strong argument for finding a traditional publisher for your book instead.

If you're aggressive about your marketing and aren't too shy to hand-sell your book to complete strangers, you can make decent money with your self-published book. However, this can be a long, hard haul. In any case, with POD technology on your side, you won't lose your shirt (or your house), and at least you don't have to end up with boxes of books lining your basement.

55. Write an Erotic Novel:

It's hard to imagine why anyone would want to write an erotic novel. The process of writing is brutal and often humiliating, and the publication and promotion of the book is usually worse. If you can find yourself a willing partner, it's far easier to just have sex than it is to write about other people having all the fun.

Have a Plan

Some people can just write 100,000 words (the length of the average novel these days) and make everything up as they go along, but that's a rare breed. You're better off if, when you start a book, you have a rough idea how it's going to end and the path you hope to take to get there.

Write an outline. It's not graven in stone. If you come up with a better idea as you're writing, change the outline and follow that new path instead.

Be sure to spice up the book with a sex scene every couple pages or so. Adding them to your outline helps you maintain a steady, steamy pace throughout the book. It also helps you keep up the variety as you go.

Keep Writing

Very few unfinished novels have ever been published. If you don't finish your book, you can't sell it. Sit down and write your first draft of your book all the way through. Don't stop to revise. If you need to go back and change things, write a note to do that later. Respect your momentum as you write, and feed it.

In the time it takes you to rewrite a chapter from scratch ten times, you might have been able to write ten chapters. And by the time you get through ten chapters, you're sure to have new ideas that will make you want to change around the first few chapters, destroying that polished prose on which you worked so hard.

Revise Later

When you're done, put the book away for a few weeks and then come back to it fresh. Although you may be eager to continue living in the story you've spun, you're too close to it to be able to evaluate it without your bias drowning out your good sense. Give it some space, and clear your head before you tackle it again.

Kill the Clichés

When writing erotic scenes, it's easy to fall back on the typical, tired phrases. If you can keep bits like "heaving breasts" and "turgid manhood" out of your text, you'll be doing us all a favor.

When you're done, show it to your friends and see if they think you're perverted—or just their kind of pervert. Get some honest feedback and consider incorporating it into your work. Or not. You're the writer, and it's your choice.

Submit

Once you're through with all that and have a big, thick, ah, manuscript, submit the novel to agents. Then get to work on your next novel while you're waiting to hear about your first.

Don't let rejection get you down, and don't take it personally. Many best-selling authors collected a lot of rejection letters before they hit it big. You may never be that big, but you'll get rejected too. Don't give up.

56. Make a Fake ID:

Maybe you want to drink before you're twenty-one. Or perhaps you'd like to pose as a citizen of the country you happen to be in. Or maybe you just need to be someone else for a while.

Whatever the reason, you need a fake ID.

Keep in mind that using a fake ID is illegal. You can make one for novelty purposes or for a prop in a film or play, but you cannot use it to circumvent the law. Seriously.

1. Scan a legitimate ID. Alternatively, you may be able to find an appropriate template with an image search online. Use Photoshop to alter the birth date, name, or whatever else you want changed. Make sure the picture looks something like you, or no one who sees it will believe the ID is yours.

2. Make an excellent color printout of your new ID. Trim this to the proper size.

3. If you have one, take apart your old ID. See if you can separate the lamination with a razor blade. Take your time and don't screw it up, or you'll wind up back at the DMV trying to explain how you've lost your driver's license—again.

4. Pull out the old paper. If you can't get it all out, boil what you have left for a half hour or so. Dry it thoroughly and use tweezers to remove anything that's still left.

5. Place your color printout inside the old lamination. Use an iron or a lamination machine to seal it. Take care not to melt it.

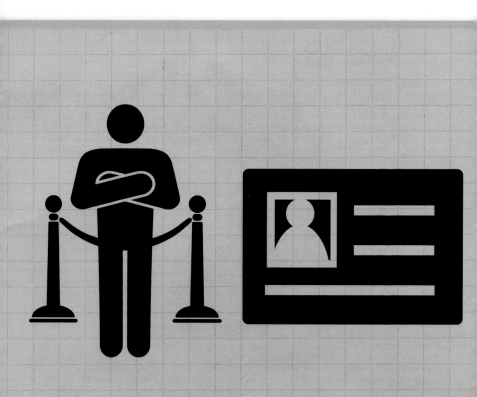

57. Lie on Your Résumé:

With unemployment soaring once again, it gets harder to find a decent job every day. It's tempting to embellish your experiences (i.e., lie about them) to make your résumé look much more impressive than it really is. If you get caught, though, you can expect to never be able to interview with this employer again.

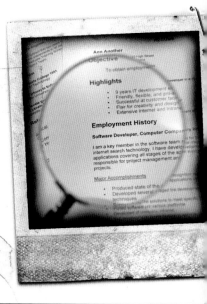

Worse yet, some prominent people have been caught after having been hired and working in the job for years. If you're going to succumb to the temptation to stretch the truth on a document that may be with you for the rest of your employment, here are some tips.

1. **Restrain yourself.** While it may sound cool to put "Founder of Microsoft, Google, and GM, holder of over 1 billion patents, and winner of more than a dozen Academy Awards" at the top of your résumé, any single one of those would be a red flag. Put them together, and the only thing your résumé will get is a quick trip to the trash.

2. **Stretch the truth, but only a little.** You might fudge your time at a job to extend it to a whole year or perhaps neglect to mention that you only held it for a few days

before deciding to take up surfing instead, but don't just put entirely untrue things on your résumé. In the Age of Google, it's easy for someone to check up on your credentials.

3. Only put down references that will recommend you. Don't include the boss who fired you. If you want to be tricky, you can put down your best friend's number instead and have him pose as your old boss for the next several days every time he answers the phone. Again, though, looking up the right number is easy for anyone who becomes suspicious.

4. Lie about things that are difficult or impossible to check. It's easy to check up on whether or not you went to a particular school, unless that school has closed. The same goes for experience at corporations that have gone bankrupt. There's no place to call or search to check up on your claims.

5. Start with the truth. While a prospective employer might accept a few dead ends when it comes to checking your references, if they all lead to nothing, she's going to get suspicious. No one's that unlucky—or if you are, you may have to be able to prove it.

58. Buy a Gun:

If you feed the need to purchase a gun—for whatever reason you may have—be prepared to jump through a few hoops. Although the Supreme Court recently upheld the 2nd Amendment as giving individuals the right to own weapons, it also said that it's perfectly reasonable to put limits on that right, like what is already done with other rights, like free speech.

Check Your Local Laws

The laws on gun ownership vary by jurisdiction. If you're not sure if you can buy a gun, call the local police department or a local gun store and ask. In many states, you can buy a gun at department stores like Kmart or Wal-Mart, so you should be able to walk up and ask at the sporting good desk there too.

Things You May Need

1. A picture ID.

2. A social security number.

3. To be an adult. If you're 18 or over, you can buy a rifle or shotgun. You must be 21 or older to buy any other kind of gun.

4. Money.

Things You Cannot Have Done

Under federal law, you cannot possess a gun if:

1. You've been convicted of a crime that carries a penalty of more than a year in jail—with the exception of state misdemeanors that have a penalty of two years or less. And you cannot conduct a gun- or ammo-related transaction if you're indicted of such a crime.

2. You're on the run from the law.

3. You've been convicted of certain drug crimes.

4. You've been judged mentally unfit or have been committed to a mental institution.

5. You are in the country illegally.

6. You renounced your citizenship.

7. You've been dishonorably discharged from the military.

8. You're under a restraining order from "an intimate partner."

9. You've been convicted of domestic violence.

The Background Check

Licensed gun dealers use the National Instant Check System (NICS) to run a background check on you before selling you a gun. This supposedly makes sure that none of the above restrictions present a problem for you.

Gun Shows

Under the infamous "gun show loophole," you can purchase guns at gun shows without a background check. At least in the twenty-eight states that still permit such things at the moment. However, you may have to undergo a waiting period that can take up to ten days.

Buy It from a Friend

The biggest loophole, of course, is that the sale of guns between individuals is private and unregulated by the federal government. If you really want a gun and can't get one from a licensed dealer yourself, anyone else can sell it to you—although this may be illegal in certain states or locales too.

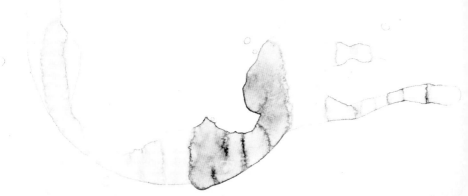

59. Make a Shiv:

A shiv is a homemade knife made from whatever you happen to have handy. In most cases, it's far simpler to go to your nearest store and just buy a knife, but when that's not an option—like, say, if you're in prison—then here's what you do.

Find Something Long and Hard

And get your mind out of the gutter. You'll have enough problems with that sort of thing in jail.

Find something hard that fits well in your hand. A piece of metal is perfect, but wood or plastic will do if it's hard enough. Even a longish bit of bone from a meal will work.

The more the item is shaped like a knife, the better. Knives have been around for thousands of years, and they're made the way they are for a reason.

Sharpen the end of this thing. It might be a metal strut from a bed frame, the metal shank from a boot, or even a spoon, but it's no good to you if it's dull. Rub it methodically against something rough, like cement, until it's sharp. Try to work on both sides equally and to make the blade that you're forming smooth. This makes it easier to maintain than something jagged.

Find Something Sharp

If you can't find something long to sharpen, then find something sharp and make it long. If you have a piece of glass or a razor blade, that's a fine start. It's hard to use something like that effectively, though, without cutting yourself as well, so you need to fashion a handle.

Fastening the sharp bit to a stick or even a toothbrush can work well. To make it stay put, you can even try driving the sharp point straight through the makeshift handle. Then bind it up with a bit of string or cloth to help keep it from falling apart in the middle of a fight.

If you can't find anything else, wrap a piece of cloth around one end of the sharp thing. This isn't the best solution, as something truly sharp will cut through the cloth eventually too, but it should let you get in a couple good stabs before that happens.

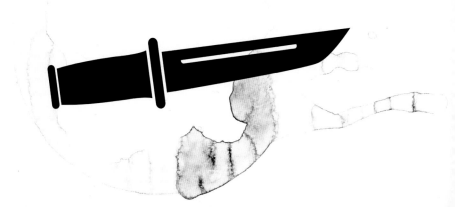

60. Kite Checks:

Sometimes you just need a little extra cash to tide you over. Or maybe you have a hot tip about a no-fail horse or stock. If you're strapped enough to try something illegal, you might consider kiting checks. Here's how it works.

What You Need

1. Two bank accounts.

2. Checks for each.

How You Do it

1. Write a check to yourself from one bank account (the First National Bank) and deposit it in your other bank account (the Second National Bank). This normally takes a day to clear from the other bank, but the deposit will show up immediately in your Second National Bank account, covering any other checks that might otherwise bounce.

2. The next business day, write a check to yourself from the Second National Bank and deposit it in your First National Bank account. This should cover the check you wrote the previous day. Again, it will take a day for the transfer to catch up with you.

3. Rinse and repeat until:

    a. You come up with enough money to legitimately cover the shortfall; or

    b. You get caught.

Penalties

Check kiting is fraud and can carry stiff penalties. Doing so for small amounts might only be a misdemeanor (which is still serious), but larger amounts can constitute felony. The maximum penalty is a million-dollar fine and thirty years in jail.

61. Dine and Dash:

One of the most interesting things about eating in a nice restaurant is that you are not charged for the meal until after you've eaten it. That's fine if you have the money to pay for the meal and are willing to part with it, but if that's not the case, you may decide you have the option to run out on the bill instead.

That's called "dine and dash."

How to Dash

Dining is easy. Dashing is where it gets hard. Here are a few tips.

1. Sit near the door. It's easier to get away if you have a shorter distance to go.

2. When you are done eating, excuse yourself to go to your car where you've forgotten your wallet. Then forget to come back.

3. If the front door is watched, look for a back or side door instead. These are sometimes located near the bathrooms. If so, you can pretend to go to the bathroom and slip outside instead.

4. Look for a window in the bathroom. If you can crawl out it, you're gone.

5. Don't sit around and wait for the check and then look nervous when it comes. Have a plan in place and stick to it if you can.

6. If you have a large group, don't just all get up and leave at once. Go singly or in pairs until the table is empty. Leave the fastest person to be the last at the table, and have the first people out get the car ready to go.

Variations

One popular variation is "Last Man Sitting." In this, the diners get up and leave from the table one at a time until the last man sitting at the table realizes the others have stuck him with the bill. It's then his choice to either pony up for everyone or make a break for it on his own.

Penalties

To dine and dash is to steal from the restaurant. It used to be that the server had the cost of the meal deducted from her paycheck, which gave her plenty of incentive to be vigilant against such thieves. This is now illegal in many places though.

Still, if you're caught, you can expect the restaurant to make an example of you and press charges, just as if you'd been caught shoplifting from a store.

— 62. Talk Your Way Out of a Fight:

Tensions are high. People have been drinking. Someone's about to throw a punch. How do you defuse the situation?

Even if you're a body builder or a martial artists, it's usually best to avoid a fight. After all, no one's fast enough to dodge bullets, and even the best fighters can be surprised or make a mistake.

Or, if you're really all that good, you might seriously hurt or kill someone, and then you have to deal with the police on top of your hangover in the morning. It's just not worth it.

Here are a few tips for stepping down the situation from DefCon 5.

1. If you've done something to offend the other party, apologize. Be sincere, even if it's not entirely your fault.

2. Offer to buy the other side a round of drinks. Nothing takes the edge off of a mad drunk like the prospect of free alcohol.

3. **Wave your friends over.** You don't have to hit anyone. Just show them how many people have your back should something happen.

4. **Show your badge.** (This works best if you're a cop.)

5. **Blame someone else.** Shift the attention away from yourself. It hurts you less when other people get hit.

Once everything has calmed down, remain vigilant. If you're facing down someone who's spoiling for a fight, they might try to get it no matter how reasonable you might be. Be wary of a sucker punch coming your way, and don't go off into any dark corners, bathrooms, or parking lots alone.

63. Dodge Credit Collectors:

If for some reason you're unable and unwilling to pay your bills, eventually the people you owe money to will start bugging you for it. As long as you haven't taken out a loan from a shark, you shouldn't have to worry about a couple of guys coming around to kneecap you, but putting up with harassing letters and phone calls can be annoying. Here's how to avoid all that.

Be Proactive

If you know you can't pay your bills, contact your creditors before they get too antsy and explain the situation to them. They would rather get the money from you voluntarily eventually than have to pay a bill collector to try to squeeze it out of you. With luck, you should be able to work something out, at least for the short term.

Seek Counseling

If you're in way over your head, seek professional help. Find a reputable credit counselor and come clean. (Check with

the National Foundation for Credit Counseling, *www.nfcc.org*, for good ones.) They will help you work out a budget that can cut down your bills and start to lift you out of debt.

If you're too far gone, the counselor may suggest a debt management plan. She'll have you close down and cut up your credit cards, and then she'll work out a repayment plan with your creditors. Stick to this, and you should be able to get out of debt.

Declare Bankruptcy

This isn't as easy to do as it once was, thanks to recent changes in the laws, but you can still declare bankruptcy to escape your debts. This is not something to enter into lightly, though, as it destroys your credit scores and will follow you around for years.

Change Your Name and Leave Town

If you can't stomach all of that, you can try changing your name and moving to a new place where no one knows you at all. Unless you can steal or forge yourself a new identity, you'll have to pay for everything in cash and forget about bank accounts, credit cards, taking out a loan for a house or a car, and so on. Even if you do become someone else, you can kiss your old life good-bye—unless you want to risk having it all come crashing down around you when someone figures out what you've done and rats you out.

64. Avoid Bounty Hunters:

If you have a bounty hunter on your tail, you're in serious trouble. It usually means you're a fugitive from the law, and there's a substantial price on your head. While it's hard enough having the law after you, bounty hunters are often more willing to bend the rules to capture you. After all, they're not worried about getting a conviction; they just want to bring you in.

Here are ten tips to keep them off your ass.

1. **Leave your clothes behind and buy a new set that looks nothing like what you usually wear.**

2. **If you have facial hair, shave it. If you don't (and you're a man), grow it.**

3. **Dye your hair a different color, or shave it off altogether.**

4. **If you wear glasses, get contacts. If you don't wear glasses, then start.**

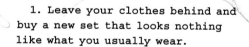

5. Lose some weight or put some on.

6. Credit and debit cards leave a trail that's easy to follow. Clean out your bank accounts and (if you don't care about credit problems) max out the cash advances on your credit cards, and leave town.

7. Toss out your cell phone. It contains a GPS function that can be used to track your location. If you must have a phone, pick up a pay-as-you-go version and then toss it out when you use up the minutes.

8. Phone people you know only when you must. Communication by e-mail is harder to follow, although it can sometimes be traced to your general location. You might even consider communicating via Skype or over an online gaming service (like Xbox Live or *World of Warcraft*) instead.

9. If you're well-known in a particular field, avoid it.

10. Avoid public events or any position that might get your picture in the paper or on the evening news

65. Get Rid of a Body:

How you wound up with a body is not important. You're just concerned about getting rid of it. There are dozens of ways you can try. Here are ten.

1. Sell it to a mad scientist for medical experiments.

2. Chain cement blocks to it and drop it in a large body of water.

3. Find an incinerator. If you can get access to one used to cremate bodies, all the better. Use it.

4. Bury it in the desert. If you're near Las Vegas, take care you don't dig someone else up while you're at it.

5. Break open *How to Cook Everything*. Get cooking.

6. Toss it into an active volcano.

7. Bury it in your cellar.

8. Stuff it inside a hide-a-bed couch and put it on the curb.

9. Ship it to China via ocean freighter.

10. Just walk away. Okay, run.

66. Establish an Alibi:

One good way to get away with any crime is to have reliable witnesses willing to testify to the fact that you were nowhere near the scene of the crime when it happened. Here are some ideas for how to pull that off.

1. Hire someone else to commit the crime. Just make sure that your proxy criminal cannot be connected to you. And that you're with many honest people when the crime happens.

2. Make it seem as if the crime happened earlier or later than it really did. Say there's a clock in the room. Set it forward a bit, then break it as if it were damaged in the course of the crime. Then be someplace else when that time rolls around.

3. Have a double pose as you. If you can't find someone to commit the crime for you, find someone who looks like you and put him among a trustworthy crowd while you do your dirty work.

4. Have someone use your cell phone while you commit the crime. Later, you can use the GPS location records for your phone to prove you were someplace else.

5. Lie. "I was home, sleeping," is a perfectly reasonable alibi for the middle of the night, even if it's not airtight.

6. Set up your computer to send e-mails out or make posts on your blog while you're busy. This can lend credence to the idea you were home alone when everything went down.

7. Ask your family and friends to claim they were with you at the time in question.

8. Hire someone to lie for you. It's best if you have something on them too, just to make sure they don't crack.

9. Pay a service to lie for you. Check out *www.alibinetwork.com* for an example of the type of company willing to do this for you.

67. Chemically Enhance Your Athletic Performance:

Not a season seems to go by these days without one professional athlete or another being embroiled in a scandal over one kind of performance-enhancing drug or another. Here are some of the things they take, and why.

1. Anabolic steroids. The stuff you use is synthetic testosterone, which helps build muscle fast. It also gives you zits, destroys your liver, shrinks your balls, drives you bald, and makes you more aggressive and prone to depression.

2. Androstendione. This hormone, known as andro, supposedly pushes your body to make more testosterone. Recent studies, though, show that it doesn't work. However, it still has horrible side-effects like anabolic steroids and can screw around with your blood cholesterol to boot.

3. Creatine. This is a natural compound that you can get from eating meat or fish—or in pill form. It gives a short-term boost to your muscles, although it does nothing for endurance. However, it can cause cramps, vomiting, diarrhea, and harm your heart, kidneys, and liver. It is legal to use, but because the FDA doesn't regulate it, it's hard to know if you're getting the right stuff.

4. Stimulants. Things like caffeine and speed or even meth can make you as twitchy-fast as a puppy on crack. However, they can also make you nervous and grouchy, which is no good during a game. Also, they can cause heart troubles, high blood pressure, convulsions, hallucinations, and even bleeding in the brain.

5. Diuretics. These make you pee. A lot. If you need to drop into a lower weight class, that might be just what you want. Also, it can dilute your urine, which might make it easier to pass when you're tested for any of the other substances. However (you knew it was coming again, didn't you?), they can also cause cramps, weariness, and heart irregularities, among other problems.

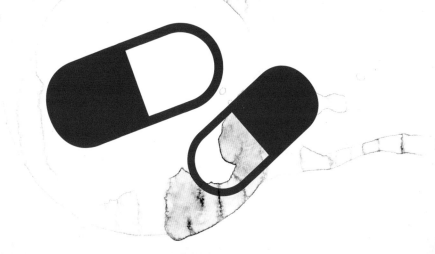

68. Become a Vigilante:

This one's easy. All you have to do is hunt down bad people and not get caught.

Know Your Prey

These people you're hunting down are serious felons who, for whatever reason, have gotten away with their crimes. (Thank you American court system.) So they are extremely dangerous. You need to research them before going after them so there are no surprises when you go to avenge their victims.

Leave a Mark

You need to let these bad people know that you mean business. They think that they can keep getting away with it because they're clever and far smarter than the people trying to catch them. Therefore you need to let them know that you're out there watching them. Whether you leave a note on the felons you've hunted down, or brand them with a symbol, you want the police, media, and other bad guys to know that you mean business and are taking back the streets.

Go Above the Law

Face it: Justice is not always served. Hundreds of dangerous, guilty people are released back onto the streets each week. Judges can't do anything about it. Police can't do anything about it. You need to do something about it. If you do not feel that your city is safe, it's time to take action.

However, you need to beware of the fact that becoming a vigilante and taking the law into your own hands is a crime in and of itself. You could wind up behind bars instead of the people that you are hunting down. That would be bad. Channel Batman and stay in the shadows, cleaning up the streets in the dark, breaking the law while you go above it.

69. Hold a Press Conference:

First, it helps if you have something to say or talk about that people might actually care about. If you do, then you're all set.

Find a Place

If you have enough space at your home or office, you can do it there. Otherwise, see if you can find some space at a hotel or conference center. If it's a nice day, you can try it in a public place like a park.

Think about where people will sit—or stand if you prefer that. Make it large enough to hold both reporters and any camera operators or photographers.

Pick a Time and Date

Unless you have something worthy of live coverage, hold your press conference in the morning. This gives the reporters enough time to get their stories together and off to their bosses. Also, you might get coverage on the noon news, the dinnertime news, and the late-night news too.

If you can help it, don't schedule it up against something bigger than your announcement. And keep it to a weekday too. No one wants to come in on a Sunday morning or during an event like the Super Bowl.

Make a Plan

Figure out who's going to speak and if you need anyone to introduce the speakers. Consider whether or not you want to take questions afterward. Reporters like to ask questions. It's their job.

You might also prepare a handout for after the press conference. This helps ensure the reporters all get their facts straight and that they don't misspell any names. You can even give them contact information if they have more questions later.

70. Become a Mercenary:

With the perpetual War on Terror in full swing, it's easy to see why soldiers are in high demand—and not just by the governments of the world. Private military contractors (PMCs) fill a real need for extra bodies to take part in various actions, or to act as bodyguards or security professionals in dangerous parts of the world.

But not everyone is qualified to be a soldier of fortune.

Get Qualified

Training with BB guns at Cub Scout camp isn't going to cut it. You need to learn some serious skills, and it's best if you've actually had the experience of putting those skills to use. No one wants to work with an amateur who can get the whole crew killed.

Join a military somewhere. The easiest choice is to sign up with your local army, although they might require a longer term of commitment than you're interested in. If you can get

into the special forces, better yet. The PMCs pay top dollar for people with such qualifications.

You could always try working with a different outfit like the French Foreign Legion instead.

Survive Your Qualifications

Train hard, stay alert, and keep your head down. You can't become a mercenary if you don't live long enough to get discharged from the military. Try for an honorable discharge if you can. The best PMCs don't want to touch anyone with a dishonorable discharge.

Apply

If you're in the military, pay attention to what the soldiers around you do when they leave. Tell them to give you a call when they get set up so they can let you know if life as a PMC is really for you. Then listen to them.

Don't Join Just Any Company

If you join a top PMC, you'll wind up with other professionals who will have your back. If you have little to no qualifications and find someone who will hire you, you'll find yourself with a bunch of yahoos just as unqualified as you. Do you want to have to depend on these people in a firefight?

71. Summon a Demon:

If devout prayers or self-help courses and books just aren't doing it for you, you might be tempted to turn to the darkest side there is: demonology. Summoning a demon isn't for the faint at heart, just the soft in head. But if you fall into that category of people and are desperate enough to give it a whirl, here's how to get started.

Pick a Demon, Any Demon

Figure out the name of the demon you want to summon. This is like getting the right phone number. If you dial randomly, you never know who you're going to get, and it's likely not to work at all.

Know What You Want

Demons don't want to be summoned from the netherworld just to chat. Know what you want from your chosen demon, and be ready to cut a deal for it.

Protect Yourself

Draw a circle of protection on the floor. Make it big enough to hold the demon you're summoning. Draw a five-pointed star inside of it, and then place a black candle at each tip.

The circle is supposed to hold the demon like an invisible prison. Don't cross the circle for any reason. And don't place too much trust in how much protection it affords you either. People screw these up all the time. Have a backup plan for your safety or escape.

Set the Mood

Start at midnight. Darken the room. Light the candles. Burn some incense. Then start chanting and petitioning your demon to pop in for a visit.

If You Succeed

If you manage to call on your demon and can replicate your success, call the Smithsonian—or *The Enquirer*. The world could use some proof.

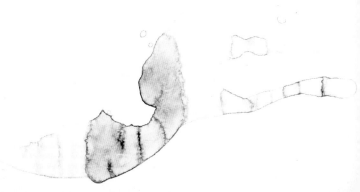

— 72. Set Up a Book Burning:

Book burning is one of the worst crimes against literature. While it's a pointless gesture—unless you can burn every copy of a particular book—it symbolically removes the book from your presence and possibly that of your community.

That said, if you want to burn this book, please feel free. Just make sure you pay for it first.

Pick a Book

Figure out which book you want to burn, and then buy a lot of them. (Apparently *More Forbidden Knowledge* burns particularly well.) If you want to burn more than one title, draw up a list to make sure you don't forget any of them.

Check Your Local Laws

Many cities don't permit open burning within their borders. You might claim that you're exercising your right of free speech, but unless you want to disrupt your event by the

intervention of the local police, you're better off just setting up someplace that doesn't mind big fires. Avoid California
parkland.

Get Your Supplies

Books burn well, but you can get things started more easily
if you soak the pile in lighter fluid. You could use a lighter
to set it all off, but it's far more dramatic to toss kitchen
matches on the pile of books instead.

Tell Your Friends

What's a book burning without a bunch of like-minded souls
to enjoy it with you? Set it up for just after dusk. The fires
look better in the dark.

Be sure to tell the local media too. You want to make a
point; you need cameras around to record your lunacy.

Practice Fire Safety

Have a first-aid kit nearby, and a cell phone ready to call
9-1-1 should someone fall into the fire. When it's all over, be
sure to stir the ashes and douse them with plenty of water.

Keep at It

One book burning never seems to be enough. Keep at it until
those wrong-minded people listen.

From our point of view, you can go ahead and keep burning
our books. We'll just make more.

73. Become a Prophet:

History is filled with prophets and prophecies, mysterious people who say vague things that supposedly come true. To join their ranks, follow this advice.

Announce Your Prophecies

Inform the public that you are a prophet. Tell them that you have much to say so they'd better start writing it down. Start talking.

Be as vague as you can. Speak in metaphors. Hell, speak in tongues. Tell people that you don't understand anything you say either. You are only a messenger for powers beyond your control.

Choose Your Tenor

Decide what kind of prophet you will be.

1. Fatalist: Everything you say will come true, and there's no point in trying to avoid it. Endeavoring to escape your fate will only drive you toward it instead.

2. Optimist: People can change the future if they will only listen to you now.

3. Pessimist: People can change the future, but they won't because they are too proud to heed the wisdom of your words.

Follow Through

No one will believe you at first, so keep at it. Eventually something you say will come true.

If necessary, you can backdate a few of your prophecies and prove to the world the startling accuracy you've shown in the past. Just don't get caught.

74. Run a Game of Three-Card Monte:

Three-Card Monte is the game of choice for street hustlers across America, and there's a reason why. If you're running the game, you really can't lose. Here's how it works.

1. Get a deck of cards. Pick three cards out of it. Technically any three will do, but tradition dictates you go with the Jack of Spades, the Jack of Clubs, and the Queen of Hearts.

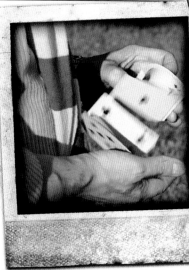

2. Get yourself a portable table. This is usually the bottom of a cardboard box stood up on a collapsible frame so you can move it around with ease.

3. Crease the three cards once each, right up and down the middle, folding the face of each card toward itself. This makes them easier to grab and move. Make the folds as identical as you can.

4. Set up on a street corner and play. This is a two-player game. You (the dealer) take a bet from the player. You show him the cards face up then turn them over one by one. Then you start shuffling around the cards until you think the player is confused.

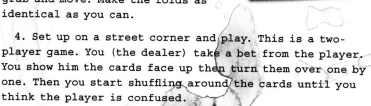

5. When you stop, you ask the player to "Find the Lady," or the Queen. If he does, you pay him. Otherwise, you take his money.

Cheating

You never pay the player. All you need to do is master two sleight-of-hand tricks.

With the throw, you pick up two cards in one hand, stacked atop each other. Then, instead of dropping the bottom one, as the player expects, you throw the one on top. This is enough to confuse most players.

If the player is lucky or good enough to pick the right card, you can foil that with a Mexican turnover. Instead of turning over the right card directly, pick up another card and use that to turn over the right card. Then, when they're both standing on their edges, you shift your grip to the wrong card and present that as the one that was chosen.

75. Disable a Security Camera:

Security cameras are everywhere. Just because you're being watched, though, doesn't mean you have to take it. Here are five ways to take out a camera.

1. Cut the power. The camera needs electricity to work, as does the recorder attached to it. Cut that, and it's done. Unless it's attached to an uninterruptible power supply (a UPS, which works on a battery backup).

2. Paintball it. You could just shoot it with a gun, but that makes too much noise. Hit it with a paintball, and you'll blot out the screen.

3. Blind it with a laser. With some cameras, you can blind them by shining a laser pointer or higher-powered laser into them. Of course, it's hard to test this theory until you actually give it a try.

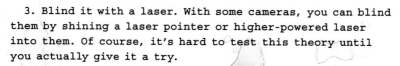

4. Slip a photo of the scene in front of the camera at the exact right distance. This is easiest if you have a photo from the camera that you can use. (Must be an inside job!)

5. Bribe the guard to shut off the camera.

76. Survive a Disaster:

With all the disasters—both natural and artificial—happening around the world these days, it pays to be prepared. You never know when you're going to have to head for the hills and survive on your own for a while.

Start Easy

You could build your own survival kit from scratch, but why bother? The Red Cross sells a whole line of emergency preparedness kits online at *www.redcrossstore.org*. These make for a great start, and the money goes to a good cause.

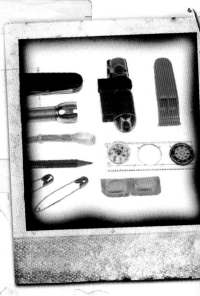

Tailor It

No standard emergency kit will fit everyone's needs. The kits you can buy serve everyone's basic needs, but you know what you have to have better than anybody. Make a list of these things, and add them to your kit.

This includes any medical needs you might have, like:

Prescription medications

Over-the-counter medications

Extra glasses

Extra contact lenses

Extra hearing aid batteries

Also pack any things that might be helpful in your climate. If you live in the desert, put away some extra water, and load up on the sunscreen. If you expect winter trouble, put a coat, hat, gloves, long underwear, and so on, next to your kit too.

77. Blow a Fuse:

You're zooming along in Mass Effect, making the galaxy safe for all that's good, when your roommate pops a burrito in the microwave and suddenly everything goes black. Before you strangle him, think about what happened and what you can do to make sure this never happens again.

It's a Circuit Breaker

First, unless you're in a really old house that's never had its electrical system updated, you haven't blown a fuse. You've blown a circuit breaker. This is a system that kicks in to cut the power when you demand too much electricity out of a circuit. Otherwise you run the risk of overheating the wires and setting the house on fire.

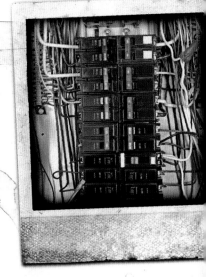

Blowing a circuit breaker is easy. You just need to put enough devices on a single circuit to overload the amperage for which it's rated. Things like microwaves and hair dryers pull a lot of juice out of a circuit, so line up a few of those, and you can blow the circuit breaker every time.

The easy fix is to remove some of those high-power appliances. If that's not feasible, you can have an electrician add new, dedicated circuits for those appliances instead.

– Other Reasons –

Circuits also break from short circuits or ground faults. With a short circuit, it's usually a broken wire that's causing the circuit to complete without any appliances on it. You can accomplish the same thing by jamming a paperclip into the two live sides of a plug, but be careful you don't electrocute yourself trying it.

A ground fault is much the same thing, but the live wire (the black one) is touching something grounded, essentially completing a circuit with the ground.

Finding these problems and fixing them can be tricky and is a challenge best suited to a professional electrician.

78. Disappear:

Sometimes you just have to get away. Perhaps you robbed a bank. Maybe you need to leave your wife. Or possibly your stint in the witness protection program has come to an untimely end. No matter what, you need to get away.

1. **Leave the country.** Go to the airport. Buy a ticket on the next flight to a foreign country. Keep flying until you're far enough away. Then walk into a crowd and fade away.

2. **Ditch your old identity.** Clean out your bank accounts, max out your credit cards, and run. Leave everything behind and pay for anything you need in cash.

3. **Leap out of a perfectly good airplane** after hijacking the plane and making off with a cool million in cash.

4. **Piss off someone in the Mafia.** They have ways of making you wish you'd never appeared in the first place.

5. **Volunteer to participate in a magic act.**

6. **Have your stomach stapled.** (Although this only makes you disappear a pound at a time.)

7. Go surfing in the Bermuda Triangle.

8. Fake your own death. This helps throw people off the idea they should be looking for you. You can even leave a suicide note behind for closure of some sort if you like.

9. Piss off the government enough to join in their ongoing extraordinary rendition program. If you do well enough, you may be lucky enough to end up in Gitmo.

10. Run away and join the circus!

79. Launder Money:

The trouble with coming into a large amount of money is that people tend to notice. If you suddenly stick thousands of dollars into your personal checking account, bank regulators, the IRS, and possibly the FBI are going to wonder where it all came from.

Laundering money is all about making it look like it came from a legitimate source via financial sleight-of-hand. It's also about converting cash into numbers in a bank account. A million dollars in bills can weigh over 250 pounds, far more than you can fit into a wallet.

Some popular ways to launder money include:

1. Find a compliant bank. Usually you want to use an offshore account for this, in a bank located in a country that has banking privacy laws. Places like the Cayman Islands, Switzerland, Liechtenstein, and Austria are good for this, but transporting large amounts of actual money there can be difficult. Once it's there, though, you can transfer it to more legitimate-looking accounts in other nations and then eventually back home.

2. Overbilling. You establish an import-export business. Overpay a client "accidentally," then request that he deposit the remainder in your offshore account. This works even better if you're providing some sort of service (like consulting) in which no goods have to change hands.

3. Invest in a cash-based service business. Give the money to someone who owns a service-based business that takes in lots of cash, like a barber shop, a plumbing service, construction, delivery services, consulting, and so on. That person deposits the money (while taking a cut for herself) and then puts the rest into the bank. As an investor or owner, you can then withdraw money as a dividend. Or you can bill the business for "consulting services."

4. Set up a personal non-profit. Politicians like Tom DeLay supposedly played this game. As a US congressman, he's not allowed to take corporate donations, but the Republican Nation Committee can. Instead of taking donations directly, his staff directed the donations to the RNC, which then sent him money for his campaign in the exact same amounts.

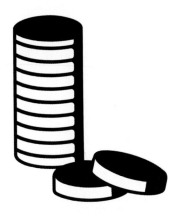

80. Break a Bike Lock with a Ballpoint Pen :

Getting most locks off of a bike isn't that hard if you have both privacy and the right tools. With certain tubular pin tumbler locks, though, it's really easy to find the right tool. You probably have a good example on your desk—in the form of a cheap, plastic ballpoint pen.

Kryptonite used locks just like this until 2004, although they've since gone over to other types of locks that aren't as easy to defeat. Some vending machines, elevators, and other devices still use these cylinder locks, although they are likely to fall out of favor as they are gradually replaced.

Get the Right Pen

Find a standard Bic ballpoint pen, one with a barrel made of white plastic. The color of the ink doesn't matter.

Pry the plastic cap off of the pack.

Stick the now-open end of the pen where you would normally put a cylindrical key. Then twist.

It's that simple.

With some locks, you may need to look around for a pen that fits the keyhole better. If you have a good fit and it doesn't work, experiment with varying levels of pressure as you stick the pen in.

81. Make a Citizen's Arrest:

You don't have to be a cop to arrest someone, although it's a lot easier if you are. Still, in every state of the US besides North Carolina, a private citizen can make an arrest in two cases:

1. You witness a felony in progress.

2. A police officer asks you to help out.

You don't even have to be a legal citizen of the US to pull this off. Visitors and immigrants of any kind can lend a hand too.

Liability

Just because you can arrest someone doesn't always mean you should. Take care to make absolutely sure you're right, or you could be held liable for all sorts of things in various law-suits filed by the people you arrest.

In the Tarheel State

While a regular person can't arrest someone in North Carolina, you can detain someone you know has committed a felony or violent crime. However you cannot transport them without their consent. (That's the difference between an arrest and a detention.)

Let the Pros Handle It

If you have any choice, you're much better off calling 9-1-1 and reporting a crime rather than trying to stop it yourself. Chances are you have little to no training in how to deal with criminals and could end up getting someone (including yourself) hurt or killed. You should only resort to attempting an arrest in an emergency situation.

Whether or not you decide to try to arrest someone after witnessing a crime, pay careful attention to everything that's happening. Chances are good that you'll have to testify as a witness when everything goes to trial.

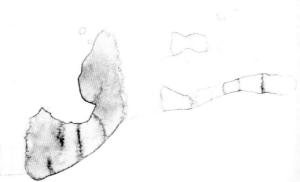

82. Stage a Collision:

There are lots of ways to swindle money out of an insurance agency. All of them involve fraud, of course, but if you don't mind that, plus a bit of danger, here's how scammers run a staged collision.

Line Up Some Help

To maximize the amount of money you can get out of this, you want to pack your car with as many people as you reasonably can. Don't stuff people on top of each other, but try to have one in every seat.

Then find yourself a doctor renowned for diagnosing whiplash and soft-tissue injuries that are hard to disprove.

Swoop and Squat

Get on the highway or some other busy road. Look for a likely target. Zoom up behind her, then move to pass. Once you swoop in front of her, slam on your brakes, forcing the victim to rear-end you. You don't have to cause a horrible accident, just make her tap you—hard.

To improve upon this, use two cars. Have the first one tail-gate the chosen car. Then have the other one swoop and squat. This makes it more difficult for the target to not rear-end the first car, and you might even be able to get two carloads of injuries out of it.

Go See the Doctor

Have your doctor friend assess you and find that you and your friends have suffered terrible, impossible-to-disprove injuries. Collect the money from the insurance company and live large.

Or fight it in court for years.

— 83. Go Phishing:

Phishing is a hacker term. To phish, you deceive people to get them to reveal their private financial data to you.

Set Up a Fake Website

First, set up a fake banking website that looks a lot like the real thing. Then register a domain name that's a common

misspelling of the actual site's name (e.g. citibank.com). If some-one happens to stumble upon this, your site requests their login data. Once it has it, it reports to that user that the site is down for maintenance and that they should check back tomorrow for help.

You now have their login information and can do with it what you wish.

Send Spam

If you can send spam to people (see earlier in this book), make it look like it's from the bank your site poses as. Tell them that someone has made a huge withdrawal or charge against their account. They need to sign in immediately to deny the charges this person has made.

Some of the better computer security packages can sniff out phishing sites these days, so the market for them is smaller than it once was. Still, you only need to fool a few people to make it worthwhile.

84. Become a Stripper:

As long as there are horny people with money, there will be others who are willing to take their clothes off in exchange for that money. If you're willing to be on the service-providing side of that trade, here's how you do it.

Get into Shape

People go to strip clubs to see tight bodies. You don't have to be skinny, but there cannot be flab. Your skin and hair don't have to be perfect, but you need to groom yourself the best you can.

Some places may hire you any-how—depending on how desperate they may be—but your tips will suffer if you look awful.

Look for a Strip Club

Look around for a strip club nearby. Check your Yellow Pages under "Gentleman's Club" or "Exotic Dancing" or just Google it.

Visit the place first. Make sure it's the sort of place you're comfortable working in. If you've never stripped before, see if they have an amateur night coming up. You can sign up and give it a try without having to audition. If you're really good, the manager may approach you afterward about working for him.

Audition

Most club managers insist on an audition. Get up on stage and do your stuff. Try not to be nervous—or at least not to show it too much.

The manager may try to get you onto his casting couch. You do not have to do this, especially in the more reputable places. Refusing should not affect your chances at the job, and if you can't get the gig without having sex with someone, you should reconsider how badly you want to do this.

85. Use an Aphrodisiac:

An aphrodisiac is a substance that's supposed to get the person who ingests it horny. Sometimes people take it on purpose, to get them and their lover into the mood. Other times, someone might give it to someone without the person who ingests it knowing of its powers. Then, when the person is most worked up, you can swoop in and offer to help out with that little problem.

No food or drink has been proved to be an actual aphrodisiac, despite thousands of years of legends to the contrary. However, there are some modern candidates.

1. Testosterone. The male sex hormone doesn't need any increase in healthy, young people, but older men and even women sometimes suffer from an imbalance that causes a drop in sex drive. Taking testosterone to bring those levels back up can get you right back into the sack.

2. Yohimbine. This impotency drug can increase the sensitivity of your genitals and the flow of blood to them. If that doesn't get you going, you may be too far gone.

3. Bremelanotide. This is a clinically proven aphrodisiac that works for both men and women. However, it also increases blood pressure, so it's not safe to use. Related drugs, hopefully without similar side-effects, are in the works.

What Doesn't Work

Recreational drugs like alcohol or pot may make you feel horny, but that's because they're reducing your inhibitions. They won't give you anything that wasn't there in the first place. They just reveal what had been hiding beneath the surface.

— 86. Persuade a Judge:

If you don't want to spend some more time in jail on a contempt of court charge, you need to be smooth. Here are ten things not to say in order to stay on the judge's good side.

1. Your slip is showing.

2. Whaddaya got under that robe?

3. I throw myself on the— mercy, mercy, me!

4. That robe really does make you look fat.

5. I'd like to defend myself.

6. I refuse to answer that question on the grounds that doing so would incriminate me.

7. Can we call a do-over?

8. Are you done jabbering yet?

9. If I get off on these charges, I'm going to find you.

10. Not guilty by reason of he had it coming, your honor!

87. Travel through Time:

While you may never be able to just jump in the Delorean and set the dial for the year you want to visit—even if you can get the thing up to 88 miles per hour—science has a few less-ridiculous ideas for how you might travel through time.

Into the Future

To get time to move slower for you than it does for everyone else, you just have to take advantage of one of the Theories of Relativity. When you're done, you'll have hardly aged at all, while apes will have taken over the planet.

1. **Using the Theory of Special Relativity, travel away from Earth at nearly the speed of light. Then turn around and come back.**

2. **For the Theory of General Relativity, set up camp inside a high-mass object or just on this side of the event horizon of a black hole.**

Into the Past

Working your way into the past is a bit trickier. You could try:

1. Going Faster than Light. If you could somehow transmit a radio signal faster than light, it could reach the receiver before you actually sent it.

2. Passing through a Wormhole. If you could find a traversable wormhole in the fabric of space and then move it about, you might be able to travel backward in time to the point at which the machines that allow this to happen were turned on. Or not.

3. Another Universe. If the theory of alternate universes proves true, you could possibly travel to another universe that's a set amount of time behind our own but otherwise identical. Or you could find yourself in a universe that's entirely unrelated.

88. Take a Punch:

No one who gets into fights, not even the best boxers ever, can prevent winding up on the receiving end of a haymaker from time to time. If you find yourself no longer on the giving side of the fight but the receiving, here's what to do.

1. Roll with it. If you can't duck or dodge the punch, don't fight it. Push yourself in the same direction as the punch, not against it. This reduces the impact with which it can hit you. But don't turn away if you can help it. Keep your eyes on your attacker.

2. Don't panic. Punches hurt, but shake it off. If you stop to cry about it, you won't avoid the next couple punches either.

3. Breathe out. Exhale when the punch comes at you. This tightens your stomach muscles, bracing them for the impact, and it also keeps you from getting the air knocked out of you.

4. Block it. Get your arms or shoulders up and in the way if you can. They can take the hit a lot better than your head, belly, or ribs.

5. Protect your face. A shot to the eye, nose, or teeth can not only mess up your startling good looks but also stun you long enough for your attacker to hit you again and again.

6. Turn to the side. Boxers put one foot forward for a reason. It presents your attacker a smaller target. This also makes it easier to block attacks with your forward arm and shoulder.

7. Keep your dukes up. If you drop your fists, you give the attacker the freedom to get even closer and hit you harder. The threat of getting hit back should make him keep a bit more distance.

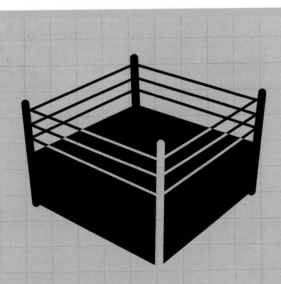

89. Emancipate a Minor:

Sometimes a kid just shouldn't be living at home anymore. Maybe he needs to get out. Maybe his parents can't take him any more. When it gets to its worst, there's a way out: emancipation.

Free Early

When a kid turns eighteen, he's automatically emancipated from his parents and considered an adult. However, in certain cases a judge can order this same effect for kids as young as fourteen. There are three ways this is normally done:

1. Petition a court. This is most often done when the kid can show that he's already working, acting responsible, living on his own, and is in effect acting like an adult. He demonstrates to the court that all this is true, and he shows that his legal guardians do not object to this—or if they do, he must prove that it is in his best interests to reside outside of their care, which is often difficult to do. Mostly this happens when successful teenagers (often entertainers) want to protect their money from greedy parents.

2. Get married. The age of consent varies from state to state, but if you're old enough to get married, you're old enough to be emancipated. This happens automatically, but it does require the legal guardians' permission.

3. Join the military. These days, the US military doesn't normally want anyone under eighteen, but back when there was a draft a kid as young as sixteen could petition the military for emancipation so he could join up. This also requires the legal guardians' permission.

90. Remove a Jinx:

So, someone's jinxed you. Maybe they called it a curse. Perhaps they gave you the evil eye. Or possibly it's something worse.

Either way, it's working. As the song goes, if it weren't for bad luck, you wouldn't have any luck at all.

Here are five ways to get rid of it.

1. **Ask forgiveness.** If you beg well, the person who hit you with the hex might be persuaded to take it off.

2. **Have it removed.** Find a professional who deals in fixing these sorts of problems. Search the Yellow Pages under "psychic."

3. **Find religion.** Most modern ones will tell you that your chosen savior will protect you from such things. Talk to members of your chosen clergy about it if you're in doubt.

4. Curse back. Make the life of the person who cursed you miserable with a curse of your own. Then maybe you can call a truce.

5. Ignore it. It's a superstition. It's not real.

91. Beg Forgiveness:

You've screwed up, big time.
Maybe you're facing losing your
job, or getting kicked out of
your house, or divorce, or jail.
Whatever the reason, it's time to
make with the mea culpa and see
what you can salvage.

Be Sincere

If you really want forgiveness, you have to mean it when
you ask for it. Don't screw around
with a non-apology apology like,
"I'm sorry if what just happened
bothered you." That removes the
responsibility for the offense
from you to the person you're supposedly apologizing to.

Express Remorse

Don't just kick yourself or say what an idiot you are. Tell
the person you've offended that you're truly sorry and show
how bad this makes you feel. This is no time to bottle up
your emotions.

Don't start weeping just for effect though. Crocodile tears and a good apology don't mix.

Offer Recompense

Say that you'll do whatever it takes to make up for what you've done. Ask for input on this, but don't be afraid to suggest ideas of your own. If you really want to make a point, you can start in on these plans and maybe even complete them before you start your apology. That way you can show that you're not just spouting empty promises but backing up your words with action.

Just make sure you won't make things worse. If that's possible, be sure to ask permission before you try to make everything right.

92. Badass Ways to Open a Beer Bottle:

You have a case of bottled beer but nothing to open it with? Don't let that stop you.

What Not to Do

1. Open it with your teeth. Sure you can do it, tough guy. But you're also messing up your dental work, and if you slip you can slice open your lips and gums.

2. Smack the bottle cap against something hard. This will most likely cause the bottle to break and will cut your hand open. However, if you do get the edge of the cap right over the top of something like a table edge, it might work without breaking the bottle. All you have to do is press it against the edge, smack the bottle cap down, and the bottle cap should pop off. But it's more likely that the bottle will shatter and you'll end up with a shard in your hand.

3. Drink from a broken bottle. It's one beer. Getting glass shards in your mouth, throat, or belly just isn't worth it.

Use a Piece of Paper

Find a piece of paper. Fold it in half as many times as you can. Five or six is usually about it.

Shove one corner of your folded paper up under the cap. Hold the bottle still with your other hand, and start prying with the paper. With the proper application of a little leverage, it should come right off.

Use Anything Else

Anything you can wedge under the bottle cap and pry up should do the trick. Again, though, be careful not to break or even chip the bottle, or you'll find yourself short one beer.

Using sillier things always sounds great as the night rolls on. It's just the beer talking. Listen to this book instead.

93. Pass a Drug Test:

If you think you might have a drug test in your future, here's a foolproof way to be sure you pass it: Stay clean.

Time Passes

Assuming you can't manage that, the next best thing is to give yourself plenty of time between your lapse of judgment and your test. Traces of alcohol and most other recreational drugs leave your body within three to five days. Marijuana sticks around close to a week. Phenobarbital and PCP can take up to two weeks.

Regular drug use keeps the traces in your body even longer. If you're a steady pot toker, for instance, you might have to wait up to three months to be totally clean.

Swap Out Your Goods

If you can't manage to stay straight that long—or if you've just been hit with a random drug test after a lost weekend—you're doomed. Unless you can find a way to swap out your requested test material for that of someone clean. Just make sure that your friend is clean too.

If you're trying to swap urine, note that most tests check the temperature of the fresh sample to make sure it's real. It's possible to purchase synthetic urine in either liquid or powdered form from a medical supply store and use that, but you need to put it in a bottle with a thermometer in or on it so you can make sure you get the temperature is right.

You can always try to get your pal to piss in a cup for you, but you should assume that the testers will watch for this sort of trick. You could also collect your own urine when you're clean, but you'll run into the same temperature problems too.

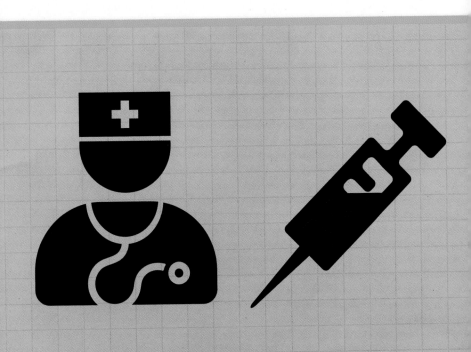

Other Tests

Testers are now sampling saliva, hair, and even sweat. Fooling these is more difficult because the tester takes the sample personally rather than giving you some privacy in a locked room to produce it.

If you're really stuck, try bribing the testing agent or switching labels when no one's looking. However, neither is likely to work.

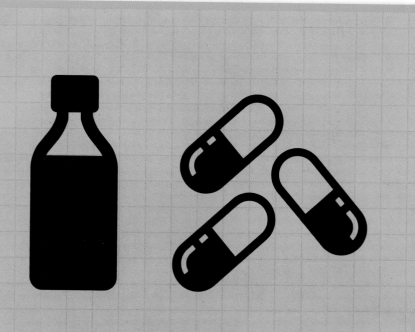

94. Be a Good Witness:

You saw something. Maybe you shouldn't have, but you did. Now you're about to be called onto the witness stand to testify about it. Here's how to handle it.

Prepare

Go over your testimony in your mind. If you can visit the scene of the event without traumatizing yourself, go right ahead. It can be months or years between an incident and a trial associated with it. It's a good idea to do whatever you can to refresh your memory.

If you're to be called as a witness, the lawyer who plans to call you will go over your testimony with you ahead of time. There's nothing illegal about this. It just helps prevent surprises for her in the courtroom. If asked about it in court, don't hesitate to mention it.

Dress professionally. While it may not be fair, your appearance can color how a judge or jury looks at you. If you want to be taken seriously, you need to show that you take the trial seriously too.

In Court

Speak clearly. Take the time to compose yourself or your answer if you need to. Listen carefully to the questions asked, and don't be shy about asking for clarifications if you need them.

Give straight answers and don't ramble. Explain yourself if you must. If you're dead certain about something, explain why. If you're estimating or guessing at something mention that too.

Remain calm. Losing your temper in the courtroom only makes you look bad.

Relax, and tell the truth. The penalties for perjury (lying in court) can be stiff, and you don't need that kind of trouble.

95. Cram for a Test:

You knew about your finals, but somehow the end of the semester just crept right up on you. Now you have less than twenty-four hours in which to shove twelve weeks of material into your head.

It's time to cram.

1. **Gather supplies.** Grab your books, your notes, and enough coffee, soda, or other form of caffeine to keep you going until you're done. If you don't have any notes, see if you can borrow some from your friends who actually showed up and paid attention in class. In college, you can also check around for a note-taking service and pay for them instead.

2. **Find classmates.** If you know other people in the class, see if they'll study with you, if only for a while. There might even be a study group your teacher put together. Join it. This way, if you have questions that notes and books can't help you solve, you can call on the others for help.

3. Get away. Don't try to study in the middle of a party. If your roommates aren't in the same boat with you, run off to someone else's house, or hit the library. You need to be able to concentrate.

4. Skim well. If you don't have time to read everything, just check out the start and end of each chapter of the text. The introduction and the summary usually do a good job of hitting the high points. Instead of reading a novel, grab the Cliffs Notes and promise yourself you'll read the real book later. Don't watch the movie (unless it's a film class). You'll be sure to get tripped up by the differences.

5. Treat yourself right—if you can. Get some sleep. Eat properly. Drink lots of water. Take five every so often. It's hard to concentrate on a test question when you feel like crap.

6. Promise yourself that next term you'll develop better study habits. It's probably a lie, but it'll assuage your guilt for the moment.

96. Cheat on a Test:

You didn't study. You forgot to cram. You're there looking at a blank test sheet with no way to fill it—unless you cheat.

1. **Make a crib sheet.** This is a tiny piece of paper that contains everything you need to know about the topic at hand on it. Write small, and hide it well. It's more modern to upload your notes to an iPod or phone, but these are harder to surreptitiously slip out of your pocket or sleeve.

2. **Look at someone else's answers.** This is tricky, as you have to crane your neck about without seeming to be doing anything illicit. You're best off to take a good look when the teacher's back is turned. However, don't be surprised if the people next to you start covering up their tests when you do. That way they can make sure you set the lower limit on the grading curve.

3. **Use teamwork.** You and your friends can work together to beat the test. This works best with multiple-choice questions. When you get to a tough one, flash a signal or

tap out a beat for the question number, then wait for the response signal. Morse code might come in handy for essay exams.

4. Steal the test. If you can get a look at the test beforehand, you're golden. If that's not possible, see if you can find copies of the tests the teacher gave out in previous years. Many teachers don't bother to change a thing from year to year.

5. Pressure transfer. If you're required to take a blue book into the exam, take notes on a separate piece of paper on top of it, and press down hard. You'll leave an impression that's difficult to read if you don't know it's there. Be sure to remove the altered page and throw it away before you hand the test booklet in though. While the teacher might not spot it now, when she's holding it in her hands, it's a lot more likely.

Don't Get Caught

If you get caught cheating on a test, you're in serious trouble. Punishment can range from a nasty roll of the eyes all the way up to expulsion. Bet on something on the latter end of that spectrum.

If you think you'll get caught, don't do it. It's better to take the test—or just not show up for it and ask for a make-up test later—than to get punished for all that.

Honestly, you'd be better off studying.

97. Play Drinking Games:

After you've been drinking for long enough with the same people, you sometimes run out of things to talk about. Or maybe you don't know them at all, and you need a way to pass the time.

Supplies

Entire books have been written on drinking games. Most times, you just need to ask if anyone wants to play a game, and you'll find people willing to teach you the rules.

Still, you can't play some games without some equipment. To be sure you're set for most games, have on hand:

- **A deck of cards**
- **Dice**
- **A quarter**

With these three things, you can play just about any game you like.

Types of Games

Drinking games fall into one of several categories.

1. Real games. These are games you could play sober just for fun. In this version, though, the losers drink. Includes: Up and Down the River, Mexican, and Asshole.

2. Dexterity games. These games test your dexterity, which is sure to become more and more difficult as the night goes on. Includes: Quarters and Beer Pong.

3. Concentration games. These games test your powers of concentration. Again, after a few beers the mind can wander, so the games become harder—and funnier—to play then. Includes: Thumper and Bizz-Buzz.

4. Watching games. To make watching anything on TV more exciting, come up with a set of rules and follow them. In this case, you're not playing against your friends so much as joining them in an excuse to knock back drinks. During a sporting event, for instance, you might have to drink while any of your players has a hand on the ball. Includes: Hi Bob!

What to Drink

Stick with beer. These games encourage drinking a lot of fluid fast. If you use wine or liquor, you're sure to have too much too fast.

98. Feed Four Infants at Once:

If your wife should somehow become pregnant with quadruplets, and you should be so fortunate as for her to carry them far enough along that they all come home relatively healthy, you may find that you must feed all four of the babies at once. By yourself. In the middle of the night.

Get On a Schedule

Babies must be fed every three hours or so, no matter how many of them you have in your home. Many parents of singletons feed their babies when the kid starts crying for food. If you try that with quadruplets, though, you'll find that you never stop feeding babies. Ever.

Get all the kids on the same schedule and keep them to it. Live your life by the clock, and they will too.

Get Help

See if anyone might be willing to lend a hand with feeding, diapering, burping, and so on. Try friends and family first, and then cast your net wider. Set up a schedule so they don't all come at once.

Get Equipment

At some point, usually at the 2 AM or 5 AM feeding, you'll find yourself feeding all the kids alone while your wife gets some much-needed rest. It's impossible to hold four babies at once and four bottles too. Fortunately, modern inventors have your answer.

Bottle proppers or holders come in two types. The first has an articulated arm that attaches to a car seat or crib on one side and the bottle on the other. The second consists of a piece of foam padding with a hole cut through the middle of it, through which you stick the bottle and then prop the whole contraption on the kid's chest.

The trouble is that babies are squirmy, which means these tools require constant readjustment. You end up having to reposition and rework them all every few seconds. Plate spinners don't have to pay as much attention as you do.

Love It

Don't complain. You have four happy kids home and eating well. Especially when you consider how badly it all could have gone, this is the best you could have hoped for. Enjoy every second of it.

99. Cheat at World of Warcraft:

World of Warcraft is the most successful computer game of all time. At last notice, this massively multiplayer online role-playing game (MMORPG) has over 10 million players, most of whom play by subscription, paying roughly $15 per month for the privilege.

When you join in the game, you'll find that all sorts of people have already been playing it for years, and they can beat you silly. How do you get even with them? You buy your way to the top.

Grinding for Gold

The currency in World of Warcraft is gold coins. You can come by these in a variety of ways, but the most reliable is to either mine some natural resource or use those resources to craft something else that people want. Often this requires monotonous work over the course of seemingly endless hours, which is known as grinding.

Once you have the gold, though, you can use it to buy what you want for your hero. But what if you don't wants to spend countless hours doing the virtual equivalent of weaving baskets?

Buy the Gold

Entrepreneurs have set up operations in third-world nations in which they pay people to play the game and create gold for them. The exchange rate between virtual gold and real cash is high enough for the managers to turn a nice profit.

If you don't want to grind, then you can pay cash instead. As of this writing, the exchange rate is roughly $40 to $50 for 1000 gold pieces.

You can even pay to have someone level up your character or to sell you all the magic items you could ever want. A top-level hero can go for $800 or more.

Cheating Is Against the Rules

While this underground, virtual economy runs rampant, it is illegal by the terms of the End User License Agreement you ignored and clicked through when you installed the game. If you're caught, you can lose your character and be banned from the game. It doesn't happen often, though, unless you're egregious about it.

— 100. Breathe Fire:

Fire breathing is one of the most dangerous stunts you can pull. Even if you don't manage to set yourself on fire, there's always the threat of accidentally drinking the fuel you ignite, which can be just about as bad.

Plus there's always the chance you'll make a mistake and hurt your audience.

Still, if Gene Simmons can pull it off during a KISS concert, then maybe you can too.

How It Works

Fire breathing is simple, although it takes practice to get it right and to be safe. It's only three steps.

1. **Fill your mouth with something very flammable.**

2. **Hold a burning torch in front of you at arm's length.**

3. **Then, pursing your mouth like a trumpeter and cocking your head back, spray the fluid in your mouth at the torch and past it.**

Voila! Gouts of flame that would put a dragon to shame.

What You Need

While you can use lots of things for fire breathing fuel, you shouldn't. Pure ethanol is an easy choice, but you can absorb in into your body without even drinking it. Being intoxicated and playing with fire is a bad mix.

Methanol or gasoline and other petroleum-based fuels work too, but they're all extremely toxic. Even small amounts can make you ill, and some of them are carcinogenic as well.

The best choice is purified lamp oil. This burns at a lower temperature and is easy to ignite.

For a torch, you can make your own or find them through various suppliers.

Your torch should have a metal handle wrapped in leather or some other insulating material, and the wick wrapped on the end of it should have enough integrity that it will not fall off when burning.

Safety Tips

1. If performing outside—as you should unless you have a building with very high ceilings, like an arena or gym—pay close attention to the wind direction and speed. A sudden gust can ruin your whole day. Use your burning torch as an indicator.

2. Wipe your mouth between stunts, especially if you have any facial hair.

3. Don't breathe any of the fuel into your lungs, and don't swallow it either.

4. Blow hard. If you let the fire travel back up the spray and into your mouth—known as blowback—you're in for some serious hurt. Practice with water until you can get a good, strong spray.

5. Pay attention to everything around you. Note nearby trees and power lines. Make sure your audience stays a safe distance away, especially if there are children watching.

6. Have a plan if something goes wrong. Keep a cell phone with you so you can call for help. Arrange for a fire blanket or a hose to be nearby in case something accidentally catches on fire. Always have a good-sized fire extinguisher with you too.

7. Check with your local fire department about permission for performances. Work with them to come up with a safety plan.

8. Train with a partner—or at least a spotter. Have this person around when you perform too. Someone has to be ready to put you out and call 9-1-1.

101. Get Yourself Put on a Government Watch List:

Write a book like this one. Just using your personal computer to hit the websites necessary to do the research to properly understand the topics you write about should be enough.

Then get your manuscript published so you can prove your claim that it was all for a book!